First Fruits
AND BEYOND

Henry Fernandez

Henry Fernandez Ministries
FAITH | FAMILY | FINANCE

First Fruits AND BEYOND: Embracing *the* Power *of* Godly Giving

ISBN-13: 987-0-9801899-4-0; ISBN-10: 0-9801899-4-2

Published by Henry Fernandez Ministries

Henry Fernandez Ministries
P.O. Box 100127
Ft. Lauderdale, FL 33320

You can reach Henry Fernandez Ministries on the Internet at www.henryfernandez.org.

Literary development by Dave Bohon/Orchard Media Group
Cover design by Lisa Von De Linde
Interior design and typesetting by Lisa Von De Linde

Manufactured in the United States of America

DEDICATION

I WANT TO DEDICATE THIS BOOK to every person who truly desires to walk in abundance—body, soul, and spirit. If you are one of those individuals, I believe you are holding in your hands a crucial key to the doorway into your God-ordained destiny. In carefully, prayerfully reading and applying the eternal treasures contained within these pages you will unlock the door to an amazing and fruitful life of abundance.

I am convinced that you were born to live out God's purpose for your life in these exciting and challenging times we are facing—times of both great turmoil and conflict in the earth and tremendous harvest and momentum in God's kingdom. Your destiny is to be part of the powerful advance of His kingdom as the days ahead unfold.

Regardless of your past, your present circumstances, or whatever the future may hold for you, you can be certain that God created you for incredible success and victory in every area of your life. But you must remember that in everything you do, it is important that you "seek first the kingdom of God and His righteousness," and in so doing "all these things shall be added to you" (Matthew 6:33).

As you read this book and meditate and pray on the scriptural concepts within, I want to encourage you to let God be first by putting your absolute trust in Him in this hour—in your faith, in your family, and in your finances.

In the crucial area of your finances, as you embrace the life-transforming power of Godly giving—beginning with your first fruits and moving into the extravagance that defines how God gives to you, I know beyond the shadow of a doubt that you will experience the blessings of abundance in every area of your life and realm of influence.

As you experience God's miracle power in your life, please let us know here at Henry Fernandez Ministries how He has met you. You can do so by mailing your report to **praise_report@henryfernandez.org.**

While you're at it, contact us at our ministry Facebook page—**facebook.com/faithforlife**—and our Twitter page—**twitter.com/henryfernandez**.

CONTENTS

ABOUT THE AUTHOR

BISHOP HENRY B. FERNANDEZ, inspirational speaker, author, and entrepreneur, is known worldwide for his practical, dynamic Bible teaching and powerful, prophetic preaching that cuts across denominational, cultural, and economic barriers. Bishop Fernandez is Senior Pastor of The Faith Center Ministries—a thriving, multiracial congregation of over 8,000 in Fort Lauderdale, Florida. He is also seen weekly on the National Network and the Trinity Broadcasting Network.

Bishop Fernandez is a visionary and challenging leader who believes it is God's will for every believer to walk in prosperity and divine health. He is committed to helping educate people to what God's Word has to say about living and walking in victory. Part of that commitment is demonstrated through his founding of the University of Fort Lauderdale, a non-denominational Christian institute fully approved by the Commission for Independent Education. The University, which was established to advance Christian education and promote leadership in both secular and faith-based areas, offers degrees at the associate, bachelors, masters, and doctoral levels.

His wife, Carol Fernandez, serves as co-pastor of The Faith Center Ministries and often ministers alongside him at conferences as well as in their home church. They are the parents of two sons, Seion-Zane and Elijah-Zane.

CHAPTER ONE

You Are Called to Be a Giver

NOT LONG AGO I READ A STORY about the legendary ancient king, Alexander the Great, that prompted me to stop and consider how we as Christians should respond in the area of giving. It seems that one day as the greatly feared conqueror was passing through a village he came upon a very poor beggar asking for the few pennies that those who traveled the road might spare him. Now, this beggar was so poor and wretched that hardly anyone would even give him the time of day, let alone toss him a copper coin or two. In fact, most often the solitary and miserable old man was the object of impatient anger and scorn by the busy passersby hurrying on their way to the town market or other places of business. But as Alexander rode by in all his grandeur, he suddenly spied the beggar, called for his caravan of attendants to stop, and in a moment tossed down several precious gold coins to the shocked old man.

"Your great majesty," gently protested Alexander's noble assistant at the king's extravagant generosity. "A handful of copper coins would certainly have been more than sufficient for this beggar's humble needs."

To which Alexander the Great responded with perfect understanding of his place and purpose, "Yes, a few copper coins would have suited this sad beggar's needs. But gold coins suit Alexander's giving."

GIVING AS GOD DOES

How Alexander's response to the beggar that day ought to mirror the attitude you and I, as children of the Most High God, hold toward giving in our realm of influence. Think about it for a moment! Our Father, who owns the cattle on a thousand hills (Psalm 50:10), is an extravagant giver in every way. His heart is ever turned toward the needs of the people He has created. Most importantly, the great gift of salvation He offers to us through His one and only Son is priceless beyond compare, taking us from the pits of sin and despair to the household of faith—the courts of the most holy and glorious God.

From there He opens the door to a whole treasury of benefits and riches that He absolutely desires to pour out on us: Healing for every sickness, provision for our every need, and a place and purpose in His eternal kingdom.

Likewise, as His children—the ones who bear His "spiritual DNA" through the infilling of the Holy Spirit—we are empowered to demonstrate the same extravagance in our own generosity. Because He is our Father, who has promised to supply all of our need according to His riches in glory by Christ Jesus (Philippians 4:19), we have the great privilege of willingly placing ourselves on the front lines of need throughout the earth, providing generously to others and pouring our resources into the work of the gospel in these final days before Christ returns.

Of course, such giving comes with the assurance from God that He will repay our generosity with all of His abundance for all our needs. "Give, and it will be given to you," Jesus promises us in Luke 6:38: "good measure, pressed down, shaken together, and running over will be put into your bosom. For with the same measure that you use, it will be measured back to you."

You see, we will never be able to outgive God. His commitment to us far outweighs our most faith-filled response to His Word.

YOU CAN'T AFFORD NOT TO TITHE!

Why is it, then, that so many of God's children have such a problem in the realm of giving? I have seen it over and over in my years as a pastor: believers come with the great expectation of having all their needs met, of receiving the gift of prosperity and abundance that God promises. They emphatically declare God's Word and maintain an attitude of expectancy concerning the great things that God is going to do in meeting their financial need.

But weeks, months, and even years go by and their needs remain unmet, and before long these dear believers become discouraged, and even resentful, at God. They'll often come to me with the bitter complaint, "I thought God promised to meet my needs. Where is He?"

I can usually clear up the problem with one easy question. "Are you tithing?" I'll ask them. "Are you giving God the first fruits of all your increase? When you receive a paycheck or some other income, do you offer to God the first ten percent through giving to your church?" Of course, the answer is inevitably "No," but it comes with a heartfelt explanation. "Bishop Fernandez, I just can't afford to tithe. I'm too deep in debt," or, "If I tithed I wouldn't have enough money for my needs."

> ***"Give, and it will be given to you: good measure, pressed down, shaken together, and running over will be put into your bosom."***
> LUKE 6:38

My response to these well-reasoned explanations are always the same: "Friend, you can't afford NOT to tithe!"

Dear reader, the same holds true for you, no matter what your financial state might be. If you are drowning in debt and unable to meet your obligations, the way out begins with the tithe. Or perhaps God has blessed you so much that you find yourself a little afraid about the amount you need to tithe. "Wow, that's a lot of money!" you might be thinking. "I don't know if I can swing giving a tenth of my income to God now. After all, my bills and obligations are more now that I am making more." Well, friend, maybe the answer is for God to trim back your income to a lower level, so you can "afford" to tithe again!

You see where I'm going with this, don't you? Let me explain more fully.

SOME OF GOD'S BLESSINGS ARE CONDITIONAL

We know without a doubt that our salvation through Jesus Christ comes totally by faith. All we have to do is believe and rest in His mercy. Salvation by God's grace through faith alone is a non-negotiable issue in God's economy. You can't give your way into heaven, and you can't get there by good works.

But too many Christians are under the mistaken notion that everything in God's kingdom comes to them by faith alone—without any effort on their part. Salvation is an unconditional gift, but other blessings God bestows on us are contingent upon our response and active participation in His plan. That is why the apostle James emphasizes that "faith without works is dead" (James 2:20). Another way of putting it is that without works, our faith is useless. Earlier in this chapter James reminds us that as believers redeemed through Jesus Christ, we will be judged by the "law of liberty" (v.12). Yes, we are saved by grace, but we all must still stand before the judgment seat of Christ to answer for how we invested the life Christ redeemed for us.

We must move beyond the realm of being merely "God, Bless Me" believers, and put our faith in action. In the first chapter of his powerful epistle James reminds us that the Word of God is every Christian's action plan, noting that "he who looks into the perfect law of liberty and continues in it, and is not a forgetful hearer but a doer of the work, this one will be blessed in what he does" (James 1:25).

You see, we are only blessed if we respond to the Word, and that means going beyond just quoting Bible verses. Now hear me, I firmly believe in the power of God's Word spoken into our life's circumstances. But there is no substitute for taking action when the Word of God tells us to do so. The problem with too many believers today is that they hear the Word, but they do not incorporate it actively into their lives. Yes, they are saved, but their salvation is of no profit to the kingdom of God, because they are passively sitting on the sidelines while Christ tells us to "Go into all the world..." (Mark 16:15). We are called to be agents of God's mercy within the realm of our influence, and we will be rewarded by our faithfulness to that call. The talents and abilities we have been given, the time we have been allotted on this earth, and, most certainly, the resources with which God has blessed us—when we stand before Christ we will have to give an accounting of how we have used what He has given us.

The apostle Paul tells us that "we must all appear before the judgment seat of Christ, that each one may receive the things done in the body, according to what he has done, whether good or bad" (2 Corinthians 5:10).

Even though we are covered by the blood of Christ, we will still be called upon to answer for every idle word we have spoken, every moment we have wasted, and every resource that we did not submit to God. Paul tells us in Romans 14:12 that "each of us shall give account of himself to God."

HOW WILL YOU STAND IN THAT DAY?

Each and every one of us has been created with an assignment to meet, a destiny to fulfill. That is why we have been redeemed. Some of us are called to be pastors, teachers, evangelists, and ministry leaders, and like Paul we say, "...woe is me if I do not preach the gospel!" (1 Corinthians 9:16) Others of us are called to education, to the media, to the marketplace, or to some other arena of influence, where we use the anointing we have from God to bring the light of Christ to the darkness. No matter how insignificant you feel in the body of Christ, make no mistake about it: you have been given a realm of influence, and resources with which to impact that realm. Your realm includes your home, your neighborhood, your church, your community, your workplace—anyplace where you belong is your domain of ministry. Ultimately you will be judged before Christ for how you used your resources and how you fulfilled your calling to impact that realm for God's kingdom.

Each of us is called to fulfill our God-given destiny based upon the physical, emotional, mental, and financial capacities God has given us, and the circumstances in which we live. God does not require us to do more, but we certainly cannot do less than what He calls us to do. The parable Jesus offers of the master who, before going on a long journey, gives differing amounts of money, or "talents," to three of his servants to invest (see Matthew 25:14-30) demonstrates this concept perfectly.

"Each and every one of us has been created with an assignment to meet, a destiny to fulfill."

One is given five talents, one is given two talents, and the third just one talent. These servants are not asked to invest what they do not have—but only what their master has given them, and they are rewarded according to their faithfulness. To the two servants who wisely invested the five and two talents given them, their master declares to each, "Well done, good and faithful servant; you were faithful over a few things, I will make you ruler over many things. Enter into the joy of your lord" (Matthew 25:21).

But how about the servant who was given one lowly talent? Apparently the master felt that amount was all this individual could manage, but he still holds him to a standard. Like the other servants, this one to whom less is given is, nonetheless, held to a standard. The master wants a return, and entrusts this servant to go out and be diligent with what he has been given. Instead, out of fear of failure and the demands of his master, he foolishly buries the talent. When his master returns and asks for an accounting from him, this worthless servant merely brings back what was originally given to him, and lamely excuses his laziness:

> *Lord, I knew you to be a hard man, reaping where you have not sown, and gathering where you have not scattered seed. And I was afraid, and went and hid your talent in the ground. Look, there you have what is yours. (vv.24–25)*

And what is the master's response? "You wicked and lazy servant," he says, and goes on to deride him for his lack of foresight in doing absolutely nothing of value with what he had entrusted the servant. "Therefore," says the master:

> *. . . take the talent from him, and give it to him who has ten talents. For to everyone who has more will be given, and he will have abundance; but from him who does not have, even what he has will be taken away. And cast the unprofitable servant into the outer darkness. . . . (vv. 28–30)*

How many of God's children will stand before Christ on that final day of judgment, saved by His blood, but ashamed in His presence as all they can offer to Him is themselves—no souls they have won to Christ, no works of compassion, no healings, no comfort given to those in need. Those believers who have lived life selfishly, heaping up riches and comforts for themselves alone, will have no silver, gold, and precious stones representing their good works, but merely wood, hay, and straw accumulated from self-centered living (1 Corinthians 3:12).

The apostle Paul tells us that in that day of judgment:

> *each one's work will become clear; for the Day will declare it, because it will be revealed by fire; and the fire will test each one's work, of what sort it is. If anyone's work which he has built on it endures, he will receive a reward. If anyone's work is burned, he will suffer loss; but he himself will be saved, yet so as through fire. (vv. 13–15)*

Tell me friend, how will you stand in that day?

SOWING AND REAPING

You see, wherever God has called you, you must fulfill your destiny through diligence. You will not be rewarded on good intentions. I have heard many individuals say, "If I just had talent I would do great things for the Lord," or "If I were wealthy I wouldn't just tithe; why, I would give God half my income and live on the other half."

But the truth of the matter is, what you choose to do with the little is ultimately what you would do with the much. There is no greater test of our faithfulness to God—and His faithfulness to us—than in the area of finances, because God calls everyone to give. He doesn't require an individual to give what he or she does not have. But He makes it very clear that your financial provision will be determined by how you commit to giving out of the resources you have—however much or little that is.

Writing specifically about giving, the apostle Paul tells us, "He who sows sparingly will also reap sparingly, and he who sows bountifully will also reap bountifully" (2 Corinthians 9:6). While many individuals conveniently ignore this truth, God attaches a condition to the prosperity He promises His children. No, it is not a hoop we must jump through in order to get Him to respond to our need. Rather, it is God's invitation for us to join Him in His kingdom advance.

As I have said before, in seeing God's kingdom come and His will accomplished on earth, there are two parts to the equation, God's and ours. Sure, God could do it all on His own—but most often He won't. He wants our participation. Our part, our participation in His kingdom advance is responding in faith to His Word, praying for His will to be done in our realm of influence, and being His hand extended to a world in need—leading the lost to Christ, healing the sick, feeding and caring for the hungry and destitute, and giving of our resources wherever there is a need.

That giving begins with the tithe—the first fruits—just as the writer of Proverbs tells us:

> *Honor the Lord with your possessions, and with the firstfruits of all your increase; so your barns will be*

filled with plenty, and your vats will overflow with new wine. (Proverbs 3:9–10)

Throughout this book you will find that I come back to this and a few other strategic Scriptures time and again as keys that will open the door to God's abundance in your life. Please understand that God can and will often meet our most profound needs without our doing anything. We do not serve a petty God who demands we religiously follow a list of rules in order for Him to respond to us. The Bible tells us that God is moved with compassion at our need, and responds with mercy.

> ***"There is no greater test of our faithfulness to God—and His faithfulness to us—than in the area of finances, because God calls everyone to give."***

But if you are looking for a portal into the ongoing abundance that God tells us is ours because we are His children, then you must follow the guidelines He has laid out in Scripture, and it all begins with tithing. No, as we will discover later in this book, our giving doesn't end with the tithe. I believe God has laid up the wealth of the nations for the righteous—not so we can have newer cars, bigger houses, and more things, but to pour extravagantly into the kingdom of God. I believe strongly that even now God is preparing those whom He can entrust with wealth, so that He can pour out a blessing upon them that they will use to fund the work of the gospel in this last-days outpouring of God's Spirit in revival across the earth.

Could you be one whom God trusts with great wealth? Will you be one of His "good and faithful" servants who invests the resources with which He has entrusted you so that He can receive a great return? As I said before, what you do with the little is what you will do with the much.

You see, tithing, giving of the first of all our material blessings, is the starting point for a lifestyle of extravagant giving into God's kingdom.

CHAPTER TWO

What Is in *Your* Hand?

PROSPERITY. IT IS A WORD THAT FILLS the mind with a whole host of images and ideas. For many it calls up pictures of wealth, luxury, and the power to have anything and everything they have always dreamed of. For others prosperity simply means having enough to pay their bills and live out their lives in comfort. For some prosperity is a right they assume, while for others it seems like a futile, faraway dream to which they can never attain.

What about God's people? What should prosperity mean to them? There are some people in the body of Christ who look on wealth and prosperity in the hands of Christians with suspicion, as if it is somehow sinful to prosper and get ahead. Flip the coin and there are others who have the mistaken notion that as Christians prosperity means nothing less than the best that money can buy. The nicest cars, the most luxurious and expensive of clothing and food, the best vacations—this is what prosperity means to them. In reality, both views of prosperity miss the mark.

AN ABUNDANCE FOR YOUR DESTINY

There is no doubt that God wants His people to prosper. God's Word is filled with His promises of provision and abundance for our every need, both spiritual and physical. In Philippians 4:19 the apostle Paul assures us that God will supply all of our need according to His riches in glory by Christ Jesus, and in 2 Corinthians 9:8 he declares that God "is able to make all grace abound toward you, that you, always having all sufficiency in all things, may have an abundance for every good work."

Here is the foundation for the prosperity promised in Scripture: God supplying everything that you and I have need of so that we can faithfully and fully perform the kingdom work to which He has called us. God has indeed called His people to prosper, not so they can heap up more and more possessions and riches on earth, but so that they can pour the wealth with which they have been blessed back into God's kingdom, financing and fulfilling Christ's Great Commission to go "into all the world and preach the gospel. . ." (Mark 16:15).

I am convinced that as Christians we are living in the most exciting days for advancing God's kingdom. The needs around us are great. Wickedness, poverty, disease, injustice, and lack are pressing in all around. Sin and evil abound. But the Bible tells us that where sin abounds, the grace of God through Jesus Christ abounds much more (Romans 5:20). Jesus, the Light of the World, desires to shine through His people more and more in these challenging days.

Friend, you and I are called for nothing less than extending God's grace and mercy into every realm of society, preaching the gospel, bringing the lost to faith in Christ, healing the sick, feeding the hungry, providing for the needs of the orphaned, widowed, and poor. As God's people, we are the solution to the overwhelming needs of this world. God has willed it to be so. As those filled with His righteousness, we are called to extend God's kingdom "unto the uttermost part of the earth" (Acts 1:8, KJV). Through Jesus Christ, by the power of the Holy Spirit, we have the authority to bring God's order where there is chaos, peace where confusion has dominated, and stability where only spiritual darkness and anarchy have reigned.

THE SECRET OF SELF-DENIAL

But it comes at a price. Jesus said, "If anyone desires to come after Me, let him deny himself, and take up his cross daily, and follow Me" (Luke 9:23). Yes, those who will go past the place of mere salvation and on to power and authority in God's kingdom will only do so through self-denial.

Now hear me well. Self-denial does not mean taking a vow of poverty, living in dire straits, and being a doormat for those around you. Just because you are a Christian does not mean you must do without and exist on the very minimum, while others around you advance, succeed, and abound. Sadly, that is a fallacy that many well-intentioned children of God have fallen for over the years, to the great detriment of the body of Christ. Foundational to our understanding of God's grace for us is embracing the truth that though Jesus Christ was rich, "yet for your sakes He became poor, that you through His poverty might become rich" (2 Corinthians 8:9). God designed us to enjoy the blessings He created, and as His children through faith in Christ we can do that even as we voluntarily embrace a lifestyle of biblically based self-denial.

"God's Word is filled with His promises of provision and abundance for our every need, both spiritual and physical."

That self-denial plays itself out in our daily lives when we love God first and foremost (Deuteronomy 6:5), love and serve others (Mark 12:31, Philippians 2:3), and give sacrificially and humbly just as Jesus did (Philippians 2:5-8). Self-denial is nothing less than giving our all every day and in every way as a sacrifice to God.

Now, let me ask you one simple question: How many Christians do you know who actually walk out their faith in this way? Yes, there are a few, but not many. In reality, it is common to see believers who are desperately trying both to hold on to Christ and the world at the same time. Yes, they want all that God has for them, they want their lives to count for His kingdom. However, they also want all that the world counts as significant—wealth, success, prestige, influence, power—and they pursue these hollow trappings in the same ruthless and godless ways the world does, fighting, deceiving, cheating, backbiting, and hurting others. The result is that they are desperately unhappy and unfulfilled, wondering why God is not blessing them.

YOU CAN'T SERVE TWO MASTERS

Jesus explains their dilemma in the simplest of terms, telling us that "whoever desires to save his life will lose it, but whoever loses his life for My sake will save it. For what profit is it to a man if he gains the whole world, and is himself destroyed or lost?" (Luke 9: 24-25)

Jesus tells us that no one "can serve two masters; for either he will hate the one and love the other, or else he will be loyal to the one and despise the other. You cannot serve God and mammon" (Matthew 6:24). Now many people think that mammon represents money, but that is really not true. Mammon really boils down to greed and the pursuit of riches. You see, what Christ is saying here is that you can't follow Him if your heart is tied to riches. You can't lay everything down for the sake of Christ if, deep in your heart, you still have a love affair with wealth.

Contrary to what many believers have been taught over the years, when you come to faith in Christ you are not signing on to a life of poverty and lack. Just a glance through Scripture will show that God has always blessed His people with more than enough for their needs and a whole lot more. Having wealth is not wrong. Worshiping it is, however.

God will allow no other lord in our lives besides His Son Jesus. In James 4 the apostle James is addressing believers who have allowed the things of this world to replace Christ on the throne of their hearts:

> *Where do wars and fights come from among you? Do they not come from your desires for pleasure that war in your members? You lust and do not have. You murder and covet and cannot obtain. You fight and war. Yet you do not have because you do not ask. You ask and do not receive, because you ask amiss, that you may spend it on your pleasures. Adulterers and adulteresses! Do you not know that friendship with the world is enmity with God? Whoever therefore wants to be a friend of the world makes himself an enemy of God. (v.v. 1–4)*

REMEMBERING HIS GOODNESS

Let's be clear about our possessions. Everything we have comes from God, and as His people it is very important for us to acknowledge this. Let's recall that God's promised blessing of abundance to the nation of Israel came with this warning:

> *Beware that you do not forget the LORD your God . . . lest—when you have eaten and are full, and have built*

> *beautiful houses and dwell in them; and when your herds and your flocks multiply, and your silver and your gold are multiplied, and all that you have is multiplied . . . then you say in your heart, "My power and the might of my hand have gained me this wealth."* (Deuteronomy 8: 11–17)

You see, God knows what is in our hearts. He knows that we are prone to wander from Him, to forget His goodness, and even to chalk up His blessings to our own efforts. He warned the children of Israel that unless they actively recalled God's goodness, they and their children would ultimately forget how He had cared for them in the wilderness, feeding them, clothing them, guiding them, and keeping them. History shows how they did just that, over and over, and were forced to face some painful times of repentance and correction.

The same holds true for us as God's children today. Particularly in America, where God has shined His face on us with prosperity and abundance literally unheard of in all of human history, how have we thanked Him and memorialized His great goodness to us? Since its very beginnings America has referred to itself as "One Nation Under God," with even our currency making the inspiring declaration, "In God We Trust." Our forefathers from the very poor to the wealthy were, for the most part, very careful to give thanks to God for all the many blessings that came their way in this land of plenty in which they found themselves. The Thanksgiving holiday that we celebrate every November began back in 1621 when the Pilgrims felt compelled to express their gratefulness for how abundantly God had blessed them as they attempted to establish themselves in this new land.

Throughout the generations, and even into the 1960s and beyond, faith in God and a humble gratefulness for His provision and abundance were, by and large, predominant characteristics of the American people. The homes we lived in, the food we ate, the jobs and livelihood with which God blessed families—none of this was taken for granted. And while not everyone embraced an active faith in God, Judeo-Christian values influenced nearly every area of society. Public schools often began the day with prayer, unchallenged by contrived legal attacks. The Ten Commandments were displayed on granite plaques in front of countless county court houses across the nation. Businesses operated on the ideals of honesty and integrity, and most were closed on Sundays in honor of the Sabbath. Even the entertainment industry followed a largely unwritten code of honor concerning what they would allow for consumption by the American public.

CHANGING TIMES

Oh, how times have changed! The America of today is notorious for its unfettered pride, shameless immorality, and its flaunting of wicked activities and lifestyles. Reading the apostle Paul's warning to Timothy about the out-of-control wickedness that will define the spirit of the age before Christ's return, one might think that he is speaking specifically of our own day:

> *For men will be lovers of themselves, lovers of money, boasters, proud, blasphemers, disobedient to parents, unthankful, unholy, unloving, unforgiving, slanderers, without self-control, brutal, despisers of good, traitors, headstrong, haughty, lovers of pleasure rather than lovers of God, having a form of godliness but denying its power. (2 Timothy 3:2-5)*

On top of our society's celebration of evil in all of its forms, Americans are now characterized by their insatiable lust for anything money can buy. Today we live in the ultimate consumer society. The average American family owns at least three automobiles, up to a dozen television sets, countless computers, along with constantly evolving video gaming systems, smart phones, and an endless array of gadgets marketed to a society that increasingly refuses limits. Our Judeo-Christian values of faith and humble gratefulness have been gradually replaced by a demanding consumer mentality. America has changed from "One Nation Under God" into a bizarre monster of greed and appetite.

To pay for their lifestyle of extravagance, most Americans are constantly trying to increase their earning power through more education, more hours on the job, more push for advancement, and more demand for ever-higher wages. Beginning as early as the 1970s, and accelerating nearly out of control in this century, more Americans now work more hours to make more money than ever before. While the average family in the 1950s and 1960s was headed by a wage-earning father and a stay-at-home mother who lived within their means, today's traditional families require that both husband and wife work at least full-time to pay the bills and fund their increasingly demanding lifestyles that put them ever deeper in debt.

WE ARE ROBBING GOD!

Sadly, with all this effort at getting ahead and with more Americans living at higher spending levels than ever before, there has been little increase in the percentage of income the average individual gives to the needs of others. While Americans have always prided themselves on how generous they are, one report by Christian researcher George Barna found that overall Americans are giving only about three percent of their income to some charitable cause. This means that 97 percent of what Americans earn they spend on themselves.

As sad as that number is, the news gets worse. Of all people Christians should be the most generous with their financial resources. The promises that God has given to us concerning His response to our generosity should be enough to convince every believer to be extravagant in their giving. But in reality, the opposite is true. Barna's research found that between 2000 and 2010 far less than ten percent of Christians in the U.S. gave at least a tenth of their income to their church or a ministry. That's right! More than 90 percent of Christians in this nation are robbing God of the tithe.

Is it any wonder, then, that as this nation has reeled in economic turmoil, with millions out of work, losing their homes, and filing for bankruptcy, instead of the Church standing up with the solution and concrete economic assistance, a high percentage of believers are among those who are suffering financially?

> ***"If anyone desires to come after Me, let him deny himself, and take up his cross daily, and follow Me."***
> LUKE 9:23

Friend, there is one source alone for all that we have, and that source is our heavenly Father. Deuteronomy 8:18 tells us that it is God who empowers us for wealth—and as we have seen over the past several years, God can take that power away just as easily as He has given it to us. Many Christians who have suffered setbacks are now realizing that they have not put God first in their finances.

Perhaps you are one of those individuals, or you know those who are living below God's standard because they are holding back what belongs to God. Because your finances represent such a significant part of your life, and because they have such power to influence your decisions and the direction of your life—both for evil and for good—God really desires to sanctify this area and to make it fully His. He wants you to surrender your finances to Him so that He can empower them to bear fruit in His kingdom, even as He is giving you more than enough for your own needs.

FROM CURSED TO BLESSED

When you make Christ Lord of your finances you are taking a huge step toward fully making Him Lord in other areas as well. But when you hold back what is His (and let's remember that it is all His) you are actually setting yourself up for failure—for a curse over your finances.

This is what happened to the children of Israel after God had brought them back to their homeland following their many years of Babylonian captivity. The temple had been rebuilt, God's order for worship and government had been re-established, and the people had been re-introduced to God's Law. But as time went by, they drifted into apathy and self-centered living, and began holding back the tithe from the Lord. God called it robbery, telling them through the prophet Malachi:

> *Will a man rob God? Yet you have robbed Me! But you say, "In what way have we robbed You?" In tithes and offerings. You are cursed with a curse, for you have robbed Me, even this whole nation. (Malachi 3:8–9)*

God can't make it any more plain than that. The first part of the fruit of our labors—the tithe—belongs to Him, and when we withhold it, for whatever reason, God calls it robbery. But He doesn't stop there.

If there is one thing we know for sure, it is that we serve a God of mercy, who is ready to forgive His children and bring them deliverance. He is the God of the second chance, and that most definitely includes offering redemption in the area of our finances. Even as He charges His people with robbery for withholding the tithe, God promises that there is a way out of the curse and back into the blessing:

> *Bring all the tithes into the storehouse, that there may be food in My house, and try Me now in this, says the Lord of hosts, if I will not open for you the windows of heaven and pour out for you such blessing that there will not be room enough to receive it. (v. 10)*

IT BEGINS WITH YOUR FIRST FRUITS

What God promised to His people Israel He promises to us as well. This passage in Malachi is the only instance in all of Scripture in which God invites us to test Him. He is so faithful and His promises so sure that He actually asks us to put Him to the test in this promise and allow Him to show Himself true and faithful. The result for us will be the same as it was for the children of Israel. Where there was lack, poverty, and want, there will come plenty—more blessing than we will be able to handle. Friend, this is the promise He gives to those who will honor Him with the tithe, the first fruits of their resources.

God wants His people to be givers, just as He is a giver. God gave us the greatest sacrificial gift known to humanity—the gift of His Son. And when we accept that gift through receiving Christ as Savior and Lord, we are empowered by the same Holy Spirit that empowered Him, so that we can be sacrificial, extravagant givers.

> ***"... it is common to see believers who are desperately trying both to hold on to Christ and the world at the same time."***

But where does that start? For the believer, the starting point for giving is the tithe, the first fruits of all that God gives us. Now hear me child of God: It shouldn't end there, but it MUST begin there. If you are not tithing, that is your first step into God's abundance and provision.

WE ARE SAVED FOR GOOD WORKS

Please be assured that tithing is not a requirement for our salvation. The apostle Paul tells us in Ephesians 2:8 that we are saved by grace through faith in Christ, and it has nothing to do with anything we can bring to the table other than believing and receiving.

But we are saved for a reason, and Paul tells us that reason in the very next verse: "For we are His workmanship, created in

Christ Jesus for good works, which God prepared beforehand that we should walk in them" (v. 10).

Yes, Christ saved us so that we can be fruitful in His kingdom through our activities here on earth. Some are called to be pastors and teachers, some evangelists, and others to fulfill various ministry in the body of Christ. But all of us are called to do one thing, and that is to give. Giving of our finances is an act of worship, a concrete demonstration of our love and devotion to God.

Giving is something everybody can do from the youngest to the oldest, the poorest to the most wealthy. What is the one thing little children love to do in church? Yes, they may make a fuss, and it may be hard for them to sit still during the music and impossible for them to be quiet during the sermon. For most of the service they would rather be anywhere else. But when it is time for the offering, believe me, there isn't a child who won't turn to mom, dad, or grandparents and say, "Can I have something to put into the offering plate?"

God created us to get pleasure out of giving, just as He gets pleasure from it. And giving as unto the Lord comes with a great promise. Here is what Christ tells us:

> *Give, and it will be given to you: good measure, pressed down, shaken together, and running over will be put into your bosom. For with the same measure that you use, it will be measured back to you. (Luke 6:38)*

Can you imagine the results if every Christian—both those who make a lot of money as well as those who make a little—would commit to offering back to God no less than one-tenth of their income? Think of the resources that would be available to send out multiplied thousands of men and women into the work of the gospel, to every corner of the earth!

Yes, the work of the gospel would go forth as never before, but something else would happen as well. In Proverbs God tells us His response when His people honor Him in giving of their resources. Here is His command and His promise:

> *Honor the LORD with your possessions, and with the firstfruits of all your increase; So your barns will be filled with plenty, and your vats will overflow with new wine. (Proverbs 3: 9–10)*

You see, when you give the Lord the very first of all your income, He promises to respond. In my own personal life the Lord has proven Himself faithful to His Word over and over. From the very early part of our marriage my wife Carol and I committed to tithing—no matter how difficult, or even impossible, it seemed for us at the time. And without exception God has met our needs, and given us enough to help others as well. Similarly, in the church we pastor, The Faith Center in Fort Lauderdale, Florida, the testimonies of God's provision even in the most difficult of circumstances would give you goose bumps!

"CONSIDER YOUR WAYS!"

Perhaps you are reading my words and thinking, "There is absolutely no way I will make it if I give away a tenth of my income." The real truth is that if, as a child of God, you are withholding the tithe, there is no way you can prosper. You are like the people of Israel whom God addressed through the prophet Haggai. The tribes of Judah and Benjamin, whom God had delivered from Babylonian captivity and returned to their homeland, began well, restoring the altar used for burnt offerings to the Lord, re-establishing the sacrificial worship God had instituted through Moses, and even laying the foundations for a new temple. But when hardship and opposition came, the people quickly abandoned God's work and took up their own, building houses and fortunes while the temple stood in decay. Their giving stopped as their priorities shifted to themselves.

And Scripture indicates that they paid a heavy price for their neglect, with God telling them through the prophet:

> *You have sown much, and bring in little; you eat, but do not have enough; you drink, but you are not filled with drink; you clothe yourselves, but no one is warm; and he who earns wages, earns wages to put into a bag with holes. (Haggai 1:6)*

Does this word apply to your situation today? Have you spent much time and effort trying to get ahead, only to find that you are getting further and further behind? Maybe you have invested heavily in your education and preparation for a career, or put your resources into a business or other investment with the expectation of a return. Perhaps you have cultivated business relationships and poured time, money, and effort into some project in the hope of finding a door into prosperity and abundance.

But in all your doing and pursuing you have all but forgotten God. You have laid aside His Word, neglected time in prayer, and put on hold the giving of your resources into the work of the gospel, the helping of the poor and needy, and other areas where you know the Lord has spoken to you to give.

What God spoke to the children of Israel He speaks to you today: "Consider your ways!" (Haggai 1:7)

BEGIN WHERE YOU ARE

It is time for you—yes, it is time for all of God's people—to obey the Lord in the giving of the first fruits—in tithing. Where do you begin? You begin right where you are. Unless you specifically sense the Lord telling you to go back and make right what you have not given in the past (and I believe in some specific cases God will, indeed, speak to individuals), you should begin by asking the Lord to forgive you now for withholding the tithe that rightfully belongs to Him.

Would you allow me to pray with you? Let's repeat this prayer together straight from the heart:

Father, I acknowledge that every good and perfect gift comes from your hand, and that You alone have given me the power to prosper. I repent of my own efforts, of putting You second and my needs and desires first. I ask you to forgive me for withholding the tithe from you, and I ask that from this day forward You will give me the faith, the courage, the commitment, and the desire to give extravagantly back to You, beginning with the tithe and accelerating far beyond. I claim, according to your Word, that You will supply all of my need according to your riches in glory in Christ Jesus. I declare that You are able to do abundantly more for me than I can even ask or think, according to your power flowing through me. And I believe that You will focus all your grace on me so that I will have an abundance of all I need to accomplish all that You have called me to do.

In Jesus Name I pray and believe—Amen!

WHAT IS IN YOUR HAND?

Now, I ask you, what is in your hand? By that I mean, what is it that you have to work with right now? What financial resources do you have available on a regular basis from which you can give the first fruits, the tithe, back to the Lord?

Maybe it's not much. Maybe it's just a few dollars every week. Let me emphasize that God is not concerned with how much you have to give to Him. He is concerned that you give the first part to Him. If you give him the ten percent of the little that you have, I know that He will make the ninety percent that you keep go further than the one hundred percent would go if you gave Him nothing. Remember the widow whom Jesus saw putting her mite—her very small amount—into the temple collection? All around her were people putting in much more than she had, including some wealthy people whom Scripture tells us put in much money. But in the midst of this group this little lady shuffled up to the temple treasury and put in what amounted to about one dollar in today's economy. As Jesus witnessed this apparently insignificant act of giving, He turned to His disciples and explained:

> *Assuredly, I say to you that this poor widow has put in more than all those who have given to the treasury; for they all put in out of their abundance, but she out of her poverty put in all that she had, her whole livelihood. (Mark 12:43-44)*

That, friend, is God's perspective on the matter. He delights when in faith you give, beginning with the tithe and stepping out and above to a higher level. If you are really struggling right now, I want to encourage you to prayerfully, in faith, follow the example of the poor widow who gave out of her poverty. If you give out of the poverty in which you find yourself right now, I believe strongly that God will meet you where you are and begin to pull you from that curse and into His supernatural abundance.

And if you have been blessed financially the same holds true. God delights when you begin with the tithe, and then commit to an ever higher level of giving into His kingdom. The old saying holds true: You can't outgive the Lord!

CHAPTER THREE

First Fruits Old and New

WHEN GOD GAVE THE LAW TO MOSES, laying out the intricate details of worship, sacrifice, and daily life the children of Israel were to follow, His purpose was far more than just providing a set of rules to keep His chosen people on a straight and narrow path. God knew right from the start that no one would be able to live up to His perfect standard of righteousness (Romans 3:10). In fact, the Bible is clear that our standing before God cannot come by "works of righteousness which we have done," but is all about God's mercy through His Son Jesus Christ (Titus 3:5). The giving and keeping of the Law was, at the very foundation of God's plan, for the express purpose of pointing us to Jesus Christ.

Sometimes as believers, however, we have the tendency to hold the Old Testament at arm's length. Other than the Psalms, a few chapters in Isaiah, and whatever other scriptures we can embrace for their inspirational value, we view much of the Old

Testament as somewhat irrelevant to our walk in Christ today. After all, doesn't faith in Christ replace the works of the Law so that we can be free from its chains?

JESUS DIDN'T REPLACE THE LAW—HE FULFILLED IT!

In reality, Jesus did not come to replace the Law, but to complete it. He declares in Matthew 5:17 that He is actually the fulfillment of all that God was promising to humanity through the giving of the Law. When we come to Old Testament Scripture, through the Holy Spirit we can expect to receive a powerful revelation of who Jesus is as we view His redemptive work through the types and symbols of the Law.

So when we read of the children of Israel keeping the Passover Feast (Exodus 12:3-14), during which each household killed a male lamb without spot or blemish, roasting and eating it along with unleavened bread and bitter herbs, we are not only reminded of Israel's supernatural deliverance from the bitter bondage of Egypt. We also get a powerful picture of Christ as God's spotless lamb given as a sacrifice to deliver each of us from the bitter bondage of sin.

As we read through the entirety of Leviticus 23, we witness a whole series of feasts and observances to which God called His people, each one intricate in God's instructions for what the priests and the people were to do to commemorate their deliverance, His holiness, and the consecration to be His set-apart people before all the world.

THE FEAST OF FIRST FRUITS

One of those feasts, to be observed on the sixteenth day of the first month of Israel's calendar, was called the Feast of First Fruits, and here are the directions God gave the children of Israel for this observance:

> *When you come into the land which I give to you, and reap its harvest, then you shall bring a sheaf of the first-fruits of your harvest to the priest. He shall wave the sheaf before the Lord, to be accepted on your behalf; on the day after the Sabbath the priest shall wave it. And you shall offer on that day, when you wave the sheaf, a male lamb of the first year, without blemish, as a burnt offering to the Lord. (Leviticus 23:10–12)*

The sacrifice, which was to be offered with fine flour and oil, along with a drink offering of wine, demonstrated to God's people that the abundant harvest they were about to reap was a blessing from God's hand. As the priest took the sheaf of grain in his arms, representing the first of the harvest they were to gather, he waved it as an offering before God as the children of Israel stood by. And as they witnessed and partook in this observance before God, they were reminded of their dependence upon God, and of their need for a grateful heart for all He had given them and brought them through.

Recall that as the people of Israel wandered for forty years through the wilderness, God had always cared for them and met their needs. Sadly, however, their response to His care was not what God had in mind, for time and again when times got tough or when it was important for them to stand in faith, they instead turned to murmuring, complaining, and looking back on what they had left in Egypt. When He brought them into the land of plenty that He promised to give them as an inheritance, God established this memorial, the Feast of First Fruits, to make certain that His people would not forget that it was He who gave them the blessings that they would enjoy. As His Word makes abundantly clear, God desires gratitude and praise from His people, and the Feast of First Fruits provided an opportunity for Israel to thank God at each harvest for His provision.

> ***"In reality, Jesus did not come to replace the Law, but to complete it."***

God stipulated to His people that they were to eat "neither bread nor parched grain nor fresh grain until the same day that you have brought an offering to your God…" (Leviticus 23:14). The waving of the sheaf of grain, representative of the first fruits of their harvest, was a testimony that they knew where their provision came from, and that their eyes were upon God in expectation of His mercy and goodness.

CHRIST, THE FIRST FRUITS OF GOD'S KINGDOM

Is there anything we as God's children today can take from this Old Testament observance? How does this ancient feast impact us today, and what is its significance to our lives of faith and fruitfulness in God's kingdom?

Friend, this solemn and joyful observance done every year at Israel's harvest was God's method of memorializing the coming day when Christ would give Himself on the cross for our sins, break every bondage and curse the enemy held over our lives, and rise victorious over the grave. Christ's resurrection is the fulfillment, once and for all, of the Feast of First Fruits.

Think about it! When the children of Israel observed the Passover on the fourteenth day, killing the sacrificial lamb in remembrance of their deliverance from Egypt, they were looking ahead to the great Passover day when Christ would fulfill His role as the "Lamb of God who takes away the sin of the world" (John 1:29). Then, on the third day after the Passover, when the people offered up the first fruits of their harvest to God, waving the sheaf of grain before Him as a memorial, they were looking ahead to that great and momentous day when the veil of the temple, having been rent in twain (Matthew 27:51) so that we could have direct access to God by the blood of the Lamb, Christ would complete His redemption of mankind by rising victorious over death and the grave.

Here is how the apostle Paul explains the resurrection of Christ, and the significance to us as believers:

> *But now Christ is risen from the dead, and has become the firstfruits of those who have fallen asleep. For since by man came death, by Man also came the resurrection of the dead. For as in Adam all die, even so in Christ all shall be made alive. But each one in his own order: Christ the firstfruits, afterward those who are Christ's at His coming. (1 Corinthians 15:20–23)*

You see, we know that our lives on earth are little more than a mist, that we are here for a short time and then we pass into eternity. The writer of Hebrews reminds us that this temporary nature of life has, from the very fall of Adam and Eve, struck fear into the hearts of mankind, who knew that their sinfulness caused a huge gulf that would keep them from God. But God's one and only Son became flesh and blood so that He could share in our frailty and brokenness, and so that through His death—and His resurrection—"He might destroy him who had the power of death, that is, the devil, and release those who through fear of death were all their lifetime subject to bondage" (Hebrews 2:14-15).

Through His victory over sin and death, Jesus became the first fruits of the resurrection, so that you and I, being freed from the power of sin, can boldly declare, "O death, where is thy sting? O grave, where is thy victory?" (1 Corinthians 15:55, KJV) Through

His victory, we are sanctified and empowered to become victorious in every area of life.

YOUR FIRST FRUITS, YOUR WORSHIP

By now you might be asking, "But what does all of this have to do with my giving? How does this equate to the first fruits of my increase?"

I believe strongly that as Christians we have allowed a huge chasm to come between our financial resources and our worship of God, and have underestimated the powerful connection between Christ as the first fruits of God's kingdom and the first fruits that we give to Him out of our own resources. I deeply desire for you to receive a revelation of how your giving—beginning with your first fruits (the tithe) and extending into the extravagance of godly giving—actually becomes a deep and glorious expression of worship and gratitude, both for God's blessing of provision as well as for the gift of His Son, the first fruits of our resurrection and victory over sin, death, and destruction.

When you obey God by giving of your resources you are actually sowing seed that will bear much fruit for God's kingdom. But just as Jesus could not become the first fruits of the Church—those resurrected through the power of His blood—without first dying, in the same way the seed you sow cannot produce unless it first dies. Jesus Himself said that "unless a grain of wheat falls into the ground and dies, it remains alone; but if it dies, it produces much grain" (John 2:24). He goes on to say that he "who loves his life will lose it, and he who hates his life in this world will keep it for eternal life" (v. 25).

> ***"When we come to Old Testament Scripture... we can expect to receive a powerful revelation of who Jesus is...."***

We know that where we keep our treasure is where our hearts will be found (Matthew 6:21). Friend, if money is your treasure, then money and earthly gain are where your heart's desire will be focused. But as God's children, our treasure is to be marked in heaven, where nothing can destroy it. God created this earth's economy in such a way that when we give that which is precious back to Him, sowing it as seed that must die, He will take that treasure that we have sown and cause it to reap an abundant harvest.

OUR GREAT EXAMPLE—AND OUR REWARD

Jesus was our great example in this context. The Bible tells us that even though He was the Son of God, Christ did not count His life as something to be grasped, but "made Himself of no reputation, taking the form of a bondservant, and coming in the likeness of men. And being found in appearance as a man, He humbled Himself and became obedient to the point of death, even the death of the cross" (Philippians 2:6-8). Jesus became that "grain of wheat" falling to the ground and dying willingly for a lost world. And though it appeared that sin and death had won a great victory over God's Son, the precious seed of His own life was not wasted.

Just as the children of Israel observed the Feast of First Fruits on the third day after Passover, Jesus was raised from the dead with power on the third day, becoming the "firstborn from the dead" (Colossians 1:18), the first fruits of an eternal army of righteous children of God washed in His precious blood.

Not only that, but God exalted Him above all else and gave Him "the name which is above every name, that at the name of Jesus every knee should bow, of those in heaven, and of those on earth, and of those under the earth, and that every tongue should confess that Jesus Christ is Lord, to the glory of God the Father" (Philippians 2:9-11).

You see, when you embrace Jesus as your Savior, you must also exalt Him as your Lord. Just as He became to Abram in Genesis 15:1, He wants to become your "exceedingly great reward." That means everything you have and are can become an extension of your worship and love for Christ. King David had this perspective, which is why he declared:

> *One thing I have desired of the Lord, that will I seek: that I may dwell in the house of the Lord all the days of*

> *my life, to behold the beauty of the Lord, and to inquire in His temple. (Psalm 27:4)*

King David had it all. He was a mighty warrior who had conquered tribes and nations and who had been blessed by God with riches and honor. But he was willing to lay these all aside and declare that the only thing that he truly desired was to be in the presence of his God, to worship Him, to know Him—to love Him.

That is what God wants from each of us today. If we will lay down our all for Him, He will be pleased to give us the treasures of His kingdom, including prosperity and even wealth—because He knows that we will give it back to Him for His purposes. "Seek first God's kingdom and His righteousness" Jesus tells us (Matthew 6:33), and all that we need and desire will be ours.

In another place Jesus assures us:

> *Do not fear, little flock, for it is your Father's good pleasure to give you the kingdom. Sell what you have and give alms; provide yourselves money bags which do not grow old, a treasure in the heavens that does not fail, where no thief approaches nor moth destroys. For where your treasure is, there your heart will be also. (Luke 12:32–34)*

WHERE IS YOUR TREASURE?

Friend, where does your treasure lie today? What are you seeking in this life? If you find yourself pursuing those things that the world values—a good job, a nice salary, a comfortable home, riches, honor, wealth—then today Jesus is challenging you to re-focus your heart's gaze on Him alone. We know that each of us will one day bow before Him and give an account for all that we have done in this life. As one who has been purchased by His blood, on that great and terrible day when God judges the living and the dead (1 Peter 4:5, 2 Corinthians 5:10), what will you have to lay before His throne. Will it be the silver, gold, and precious stones of a life lived for Him, giving your all in extravagance to Him? Or will you be saved "as by fire" (1 Corinthians 3:15), having nothing of eternal value that you have accomplished for God's kingdom?

No, the kingdom of God is not all about money, and, of course, God does not need your resources to accomplish His kingdom purposes. But He does want your heart, He wants to be your treasure and your "exceedingly great reward."

How you weigh your financial resources—the treasure God has given you in this world—against His far greater eternal economy is a very accurate barometer of where your heart truly is. That is why God wants you to give Him the first and the best of all with which He has blessed you. When you honor Him with the first fruits of all your increase, you are embracing in one of the most practical ways the principle of seeking first the kingdom of God. Your are sowing your seed in the good ground that God has prepared from the foundations of the earth.

Just as the Old Testament Feast of First Fruits was a celebration both of the blessing of the material harvest as well as of the coming harvest that Christ would accomplish, so today we can celebrate in the same way every time we give the tithe—the first fruits of our increase. Our giving becomes a living memorial and expression of gratitude of God's promised blessing and of the harvest of souls that will continue until Christ returns.

If you will view your first fruits giving in this way, I guarantee that two things will happen: 1) you will always have sufficient abundance for both your needs as well as those in your realm of influence; and 2) there will be an abundance of resources for the work of the kingdom—for winning people to Christ, discipling them into maturity, equipping them both materially and spiritually, and releasing them into their kingdom destiny.

CHAPTER FOUR

Getting Our Priorities Right

AS I WRITE THESE WORDS, men and women all over America are preparing for that day of reckoning that comes on April 15th every year: Tax day. For some it is no big deal. They know that they've paid in enough throughout the preceding months so there will be no surprises when they fill out their annual returns. For others the day brings great stress and uncertainty as they calculate just how much of their hard-earned income Uncle Sam will take for his own purposes—and how they will scrape up enough to pay what local, state, and federal government demands.

For each and every one of us, paying taxes represents a huge priority. We work hard throughout the months to pay our bills, put food on the table, and provide for ourselves and our families. But even as we work, save, and plan for our financial future, we know that once a year there is a day of judgment that we must face. It comes like clockwork, and we know that it is a priority that we ignore at our peril.

THE KINGDOM PRIORITY

Life is filled with many such priorities. It seems that no matter where we turn, someone or something is demanding a piece of our time, our resources, and our lives. School, careers, family, relationships of all kinds outside the home, and a whole host of obligations seem to come against us from the day we are born, chipping away at our very being and killing us a little each day.

There is a priority in our lives, however, that does just the opposite, building us up, giving us life, and refreshing us in every way. It is a priority like no other—the most crucial and transforming priority to which we can give ourselves—and make no mistake, we are called to make it number one in our lives.

Of course, I am referring to God's kingdom, which is the source of all our needs, desires, dreams, and of our very destiny. When we answer the call of Christ, making Him both Savior and Lord, we are saying yes to the highest life priority that God has created. But unlike those obligations that rob us of energy and strength, embracing the priority of God's kingdom will lead us to an unending fountain of living water that gives us life in every circumstance, no matter how trying. When we say yes to Christ we are accepting His great invitation:

> *Come to Me, all you who labor and are heavy laden, and I will give you rest. Take My yoke upon you and learn from Me, for I am gentle and lowly in heart, and*

you will find rest for your souls. For My yoke is easy and My burden is light. (Matthew 11: 28-30)

Learning from Jesus, getting a revelation of His glory and power, will change how you think about everything in life. I am talking about Holy Spirit-inspired revelation. I used to think that "learning from Christ" was all about my putting in enough time in the Word, in prayer, and at church. It was all about what I did. But truly becoming what God created you to be goes beyond just putting in time and going through the motions of a righteous lifestyle.

Each one of us must make a commitment that goes beyond our feelings and emotions to enter into the rest of Christ, sit at His feet, take on His image, and be transformed into His likeness.

SEEKING GOD WITH YOUR RESOURCES

Don't get me wrong. That will include giving yourself to God's Word and to prayer, making communion with God your highest priority. But it will go beyond just going through the motions to defining every area of your life—including how you invest your time and your resources.

This goes to the heart of what Jesus meant when He said to "seek first the kingdom of God and His righteousness" (Matthew 6:33). God knows all the things that we need in life (Matthew 6:8), and He is searching for those who will lay down those needs before Him and focus on His kingdom first. This is the core of firstfruits giving.

Sadly, too many of God's people do the opposite. Yes, they ask God for His provision, but then they spend all of their energy stressing out about how they are going to have enough to meet their needs, and they pull up short in giving of their tithes and offerings. Believe me, I am not downplaying the incredible financial stress with which many are burdened today. With so many people unemployed—or underemployed—and with the economy seemingly tottering on the edge of collapse, these are times of great stress for countless thousands of individuals and families.

> ***"When we answer the call of Christ . . . we are saying yes to the highest life priority that God has created."***

But God's people are not doomed to failure and defeat, and even in the most trying of times this world faces God promises that He will supply all of our needs "according to His riches in glory by Christ Jesus" (Philippians 4:19). Stepping out in faith and giving your best in the times of blessing as well as in times of need is a declaration to God—as well as before the powers of darkness—that you are taking God at His Word, and that you are fully persuaded that when you are faithful in the tithe He will pour out on your life such a blessing that you will not be able to contain it (Malachi 3:10).

Friend, in your life, faith can triumph over fear and you can discover that place of God's riches and provision for all that

God has called you to do. You may have to persevere and stand through some times of trial and testings. All visible means of provision may even dry up, as this world faces famine, pestilence, and times of great need. But God has promised that He will never leave or forsake you, and that means in your specific circumstances you can rest in His care and provision.

A NEVER ENDING SUPPLY

There is an unforgettable story in 1 Kings 17 that perfectly illustrates God's provision for those who put kingdom giving first. It is really a story of two individuals from two very different walks of life, each of whom is faced with the opportunity to put God's kingdom before their own needs, and who experience His abundant, miraculous provision.

First we see Elijah, a prophet of God sent to restore order to the nation of Israel. As he stands righteously before Israel's King Ahab, boldly declaring the Word of the Lord, he must also withstand the wicked Jezebel and her 450 godless prophets of Baal. Through it all we observe as God faithfully supplies all of Elijah's needs according to His riches. No, He doesn't do it by giving the prophet a fat checking account to draw on as he travels through the country giving a strong word of God's judgment. Elijah is impacted by the drought just like everyone else, even though he is faithfully obeying God. We even witness Elijah's courage tested and see him assailed by fear as the wicked Jezebel vows to destroy him for executing her godless prophets and cleansing the land of the wickedness of Baal worship.

But through all the circumstances of His life—a life in which He has made God's kingdom a priority—Elijah finds God faithful to His Word. You see, not only does God own the cattle on a thousand hills, but he controls the very birds of the air and every living thing. So it is nothing for him to feed Elijah by having Ravens bring him bread and meat every morning and evening (1 Kings 17:6), by having an angel miraculously bring him bread and water as he hides from the wicked wrath of Jezebel (1 Kings 19: 5-8)—or by speaking to a destitute widow who is down to just enough flour and oil to make a final simple meal for herself and her son before they give up and die of starvation.

FIRST FRUITS IN ACTION

In the example of the widow of Zarephath we see the principle of first fruits in action. Here was a woman whose very life was on the line when the prophet Elijah first encountered her gathering sticks for the small fire to cook what she thought would be her last meal. No doubt her mind was wracked by apprehension and fear. She had cried out to God for deliverance from the poverty that was about to overtake her and her precious son. But there appeared to be no help in sight.

Into this hopeless situation God was about to break through with abundance. But it would take a step of faith on the part of the woman. You see, God had already prepared the prophet to bring the Word of the Lord to this woman in her despair. In 1 Kings 17 we read that the drought which God had sent against Israel for their sin had dried up the brook where Elijah was camped out, and where God had been providing miraculously for his daily needs. With no water, Elijah was forced to move on, trusting God to show him where he should go. Into Elijah's tough circumstances God speaks specific direction, "Arise, go to Zarephath . . . and dwell there. See, I have commanded a widow there to provide for you" (v. 9).

Just how the Lord had informed this desperate woman that she would be the conduit of God's blessing in the prophet's life Scripture does not relate. But I can well imagine the doubt that filled her mind as she left her house that morning, with no clue as to how she would take care of herself and her son, let alone an extra mouth that God was sending her to feed.

But I can attest that this is how God often moves as He prepares to break into impossible situations in people's lives. The Bible tells us that God desires unwavering faith in his people (Hebrews 11: 6), and He will keep placing us in situations that challenge us as we learn to trust Him.

"In the example of the widow of Zarephath we see the principle of first fruits in action."

As Elijah came to the gates of the city he immediately saw the widow gathering sticks, and called out to her, "Please bring me a little water in a cup, that I may drink" (v. 10). And as she turned to get the water, Elijah added the command that God would use to test this woman's faith, "Please bring me a morsel of bread in your hand" (v. 11).

The widow's response to Elijah's request is thought-provoking, because it demonstrates the doubt that was in her mind at what the prophet—and the Lord—were asking of her:

> *As the Lord your God lives, I do not have bread, only a handful of flour in a bin, and a little oil in a jar; and see, I am gathering a couple of sticks that I may go in and prepare it for myself and my son, that we may eat it, and die. (v. 12)*

"TRY ME NOW IN THIS"

Just as this woman was living in the middle of a famine, today there are countless believers who are struggling in the midst of a financial famine, and the idea of giving the first fruits of what little they have is almost too much to face. Let me emphasize here that God perfectly understands this. If you are facing such circumstances, God is not standing ready to condemn your apprehension and doubt about the wisdom of giving out of your poverty. He understands where you are at.

But He loves you too much to allow you to opt out of this divinely commissioned opportunity for Him to prove His faithfulness in your life. "Try me now in this," God is declaring to you, "and see if I will not bless your step of faith by pouring out a blessing so large that you will not be able to contain it" (Malachi 3:10, paraphrase).

Giving of the first fruits of all your increase—regardless of how much or how little you have—is an open door from God that will lead directly into His blessings for your every need. I want to encourage you to battle through the doubt, chip away at any apprehensions, and rise above all reservations you harbor about obeying God in the giving of your tithes and your offerings. In fact, I challenge you that if you have to, give even in spite of your doubt, because in doing so you will be demonstrating faith to God and defiance to the devil, declaring boldly that "I believe my God shall supply all of my needs abundantly, according to His riches in glory by Christ Jesus."

GOD WILL NOT FAIL YOU

As the widow expressed her own reservations about giving her first—as well as her last—to the man of God, a word from the Lord came to her from the prophet—a word, no doubt, confirming the command God had given to her earlier to provide for Elijah's needs:

> *Do not fear; go and do as you have said, but make me a small cake from it first, and bring it to me; and afterward make some for yourself and your son. For thus says the Lord God of Israel: "The bin of flour shall not be*

used up, nor shall the jar of oil run dry, until the day the Lord sends rain on the earth." (vv.13-14)

God's Word relates that as the widow stepped out in faith and gave to God the first of what she had, the Lord responded to her faith with miraculous power and provision. From that day forward, her bin of flour and her jar of oil were replenished even as those around her suffered under the famine. Each day as she turned to her daily chore of providing a meal for her son, herself, and the prophet, God multiplied what she had, so there was more than enough. Just as He would later do with the loaves and the fishes by the Sea of Galilee, He multiplied the food this woman had so that she had "an abundance for every good work" to which God had called her (2 Corinthians 9:8).

GOD IS STILL WORKING

This is not just a story of long ago and far away. It happens even in our modern world. I am reminded of the miraculous account of a Swedish missionary by the name of Gösta Öman, who was serving the people of South Korea back in the 1960s. This was in the middle of a severe food shortage in the country, and when Gösta and his wife, a doctor, would rise in the morning they would often find outside their door, on the path to town, the body of at least one person who had died of starvation in the night.

The tragedy was so overwhelming that Gösta began praying fervently for a miracle that might allow him to feed the scores of peasants and families who came to his door each day, asking for something to eat. I am sure his prayers were all very rational, asking God for a load of food aboard a cargo ship from home or America.

Instead, as Gösta was in an intense time of prayer for the great need, the Lord suddenly spoke to this man of God to purchase a 170-pound bag of rice from the local market, to pour it into his wooden household rice bin, and then to give freely to whoever showed up at his door in need.

As Gösta reflected upon the enormity of what God was asking him to do, he began to blurt out, "But God, this is IMPOSSIB . . ."—but God would not let him finish.

"What I have called you to do, I will empower you to do," God spoke clearly to this servant of God, who had given all to come and minister to the needy people of Korea. With the assurance that "with God all things are possible" (Matthew 19:26), Gösta obeyed the Lord, purchased the bag of rice, and soon news spread around the area that there was food at the missionary's house.

Gösta recalled that before long there was a long line of people from morning to night who came to receive the Lord's blessing, and he estimated that over the next six months he dispensed over 100 tons of rice from that one bag poured into his rice bin. You see, just as the bin of flour and the jar of oil never failed for the widow of Zarapheth, in the same way the bin of rice never failed for Gösta. God was faithful!

When we put God first, when we give Him the first fruits of all that is ours—whether that means our finances, our time, our efforts, or other resources—He will always give back "pressed down shaken together, and running over."

A PERSONAL STORY

God has shown himself faithful to me personally in this very way. When my wife Carol and I first moved to Florida, let me tell you it was a big stretch of our faith. We had given our lives to church and ministry and really didn't have much more to give. This was before God revealed His plan for The Faith Center, Henry Fernandez Ministries, and the University of Fort Lauderdale, and we moved to this new place totally by faith, following Him and waiting for His direction.

But we still had to eat, we had no money, and I remember praying one night and wrestling with just what I should do to put food on the table. I reminded God (as if He needed my help remembering) of His promise to supply all of our needs, and as I waited on Him I felt clearly that He wanted me to step out, go to the grocery store—with no money in my wallet—get the things we needed, and allow Him to supply the money to pay the bill when we got up to the checkout counter.

With a combination of faith and more than a little apprehension, Carol and I made our way to the local grocery store, and as the Holy Spirit had directed in prayer, we pushed our shopping cart up and down the isles, picking out our groceries—without a dollar to our names.

But let me assure you that even in my apprehension my heart was full of faith that what God had directed me to do He would help me fulfill. You see, God isn't into embarrassing His children. He gets no thrill out of our failures. Instead, He gets great joy when He sees us step out in faith, trusting Him to see us through. He loves to prove Himself faithful in those situations.

When Carol and I got to the checkout counter, with a cart full of groceries and no way to pay, I have to admit I felt a little nervous. I think I understand, just a little bit, what that widow felt like making a meal for Elijah with no visible means of providing for her and her son—even though God had said He would meet the need.

As we began putting our groceries on the conveyor belt and the checkout lady tallied our bill, a man walked into the grocery store, came straight up to me, and said, "I was sleeping, and the Holy Spirit woke me up and told me, 'Henry is at the Winn-Dixie grocery store. Take him some money.' So here I am."

> ***"...godliness with contentment is great gain."***
> 1 TIMOTHY 6:6

Friend, the role of bills this gentleman handed me was far more than we needed for our groceries. In fact, when God had told me to go shopping, he was offering me a blank check inviting me to "go for it" and fill my cart. He wanted to give us an abundance, but I held back as though I thought the chances of God providing for us were higher if I only took the basics.

The law of the first fruits is "pressed down, shaken together, and running over." Believe me, I learned my lesson that day, and since then I have always believed God for the best, not "just enough."

TOTAL PROVISION, ABUNDANT SUPPLY

God is no respecter of persons. What He did for Elijah and the widow, what He did for the Swedish missionary, Gösta Öman, back in the 1960s, and what He did for my wife and me as we stepped out into a new chapter of our lives, He will most certainly do for you.

You may be facing a famine of your own right now, just as many thousands of individuals are all over the nation—and the world. Many are ready to give up in despair because they have lost their livelihood and a standard of living they were used to. Perhaps you are in that very place yourself. But it is important to remember that God has not forsaken you, and even in the difficult place of financial famine God will take care of you in a miraculous and abundant way.

Now be advised, God didn't supply the widow with a huge bank account, or by stocking her pantry with an overflowing of goods. And He may not choose to do that for you, either. We have lived so long in a culture of excess, that we have come to equate excess with abundance. I believe God is working in the lives of many people today, redefining for them what His prosperity and provision mean in their lives.

The apostle Paul defines prosperity for the child of God as "having all sufficiency in all things" so that you may have "an abundance for every good work" (2 Corinthians 9:8). What exactly does that mean? I believe it means that in every situation in which we find ourselves as God's children, we will always have more than enough. As an apostle Paul found himself in many different circumstances, both of abundance and need. God taught him how to live joyfully either way, knowing that God would empower him to succeed:

> *I know how to be abased, and I know how to abound. Everywhere and in all things I have learned both to be full and to be hungry, both to abound and to suffer need. I can do all things through Christ who strengthens me. (Philippians 4:12-13)*

Now hear me well. The great apostle was not trying to say that he enjoyed doing without, or that it was his goal as a man of God to be abased and hungry. Far from it! What he was saying is that in trusting God fully he was able to lay down the expectation of having his needs laid out nicely for him on a daily basis. Instead he could rest in the absolute knowledge that his God would always supply his needs out of His great storehouse, while Paul gave himself to the work of the gospel.

LEARNING CONTENTMENT

In 1 Timothy, Paul offers another Holy Spirit-inspired revelation of what true abundance is all about to the child of God, telling us that "godliness with contentment is great gain. For we brought nothing into this world, and it is certain we can carry nothing out. And having food and clothing, with these we shall be content" (1 Timothy 6: 6-8).

How different that is from the attitude the world tries to foist upon us. From the earliest age most individuals, particularly in America, are conditioned to be anything but content. From television to movies to what they learn at school, kids and young people today are taught to demand ever more of the best that this world has to offer. And when they grow up this demanding attitude turns into one of restlessness and discontent, with people spending their whole lives searching desperately for something that will satisfy them.

The saddest part of this is the extent to which this mind-set has crept into the church and into the thoughts and motives of God's people. Yet all the while God keeps trying to get the attention of His children, telling them, "Be content with what I have given you. My presence and provision are enough for you, because I will never leave or forsake you" (Hebrews 13:5, paraphrase).

Friend, true prosperity in God's kingdom goes far beyond mere money. That is why God wants us to have an open hand with our resources, because he knows that money alone can never make us happy. Paul tells us that "God loves a cheerful giver" (2 Corinthians 9: 7), and that is a fundamental principle tied to prosperity in God's kingdom—and is a secret of first fruits giving.

PROSPERITY FROM THE INSIDE OUT

You see, true prosperity is something that happens from the inside out. You can never truly be prosperous in God's kingdom until you un-attach your happiness from what you have. If you give with a cheerful heart you will most likely give abundantly, and you will receive back in kind. Likewise, if you give begrudgingly you are most likely to give stingily—and, consequently, your harvest will be meager.

God does not want our identity and our happiness tied up in what we have here on earth, but what we have in heaven. Riches and possessions have a tendency to distract us from what our focus as Christians should be: loving God and loving and serving others. The apostle Paul explains it this way:

> *. . . those who desire to be rich fall into temptation and a snare, and into many foolish and harmful lusts which drown men in destruction and perdition. For the love of money is a root of all kinds of evil, for which some have strayed from the faith in their greediness, and pierced themselves through with many sorrows. (1 Timothy 6:6–9)*

That doesn't mean it is wrong to be wealthy. I know a few very wealthy individuals who are happy, carefree, generous, and blessed beyond measure. That is because they do not love money. Instead, they love God and it shows in what they do with their wealth.

Just as Jesus tells us, they have learned not to fear, knowing that it is the Father's good will to give them the kingdom (Luke 12:32). And they have taken to heart Christ's counsel:

> *Sell what you have and give alms; provide yourselves money bags which do not grow old, a treasure in the heavens that does not fail, where no thief approaches nor moth destroys. For where your treasure is, there your heart will be also. (vv. 33–34)*

Friend, as God's child have you settled the question of what you will value here on earth? I am saddened by how often God has to pry the things of this world from the fingers of His children, so that He can adjust their focus onto their true treasure, the One who gave His all for them and the only One who is worthy of their worship and devotion.

> ***"... where your treasure is, there your heart will be also."***

Even now as so many individuals are struggling with financial issues, losing jobs, homes, income, and a lifestyle they have worked so diligently to build, the Holy Spirit is speaking tenderly to them to just let it all go and turn their heart's gaze upon Christ alone. Believe me, it is not because God doesn't want them to have the things they need to live, or that He doesn't want them to prosper in this life. Rather, He wants each of us to learn that true prosperity comes from the inside out.

GOD'S WORD BRINGS FREEDOM

In 3 John we read these words from the apostle: "Beloved, I pray that you may prosper in all things and be in health, just as your soul prospers" (3 John 2). You see, as God's children our prosperity must begin with what is inside us. It doesn't begin with a good education, followed by a good job and promotion at the hands of men. That is where so many believers lose their way. They pray and seek after these things while right at their fingertips is the one thing that will bring them true prosperity, a deep and lasting relationship with Jesus, founded upon the Word of God.

Friend, the truth of God's Word will being freedom to every area of your life, because in it you will get a true revelation of Jesus Christ, you will be conformed to His image, and you will be empowered to do the kingdom works that He did—and yes, greater works will you do, just as He promised, because you have His Holy Spirit within you (John 14: 12).

If you are searching for true prosperity in your life, then I want to encourage you to get into the depths of God's Word on a daily basis, searching out what God says about who you are as His child, who His Son is in your life, and how His truth fits into your daily walk. As His child you do not have to walk around in confusion when the riches of His Word are there for you to embrace for your life.

As you give yourself to God's Word, you will experience true prosperity in every way—body, soul, and spirit. You will find His abundance literally chasing you down in your circumstances. You will find yourself the recipient of healing in every corner of your existence. As I have said for years, true prosperity will make it so that there is nothing broken and nothing missing in your life.

Will there be trials and testings? Certainly! Will the enemy challenge you and try to strip you of what God has given you? Absolutely! Will others try to undermine the blessings that seem to overtake you on a daily basis? There is no doubt about it. Jesus said that there is no one who has laid down his or her life for the kingdom of God who will not receive an abundance of prosperity, but that prosperity will come "with persecutions" (Mark 10:30).

Will you have to stand firm in the things that God has called you to do, in the places God has called you to go, and in the ground that God has called you to take for His sake? Will you be called to do spiritual warfare for your destiny of abundance? Yes you will, just as Christ tells us that the kingdom of heaven "suffers violence, and the violent take it by force" (Matthew 11: 12).

Now, the violence that Jesus is talking about here is not the kind that will hurt or destroy others, either physically or emotionally. It is not about the words you say to put others in their place, to make sure people know where you stand, or to establish your turf and territory. No, the violence Jesus is referring to is the kind that will tear down spiritual strongholds and obstacles, that will destroy the works of the enemy, and that will take the territory that God says in His Word belongs to you as His child. It is the kind of violence whereby you will take up the sword of the spirit, which is the Word of God (Ephesians 6:17).

God says that His Word, in your heart and in your mouth, "is living and powerful, and sharper than any two-edged sword, piercing even to the division of soul and spirit, and of joints and marrow, and is a discerner of the thoughts and intents of the heart" (Hebrews 4:12).

So when you give yourself to His Word, your heart and mind will be renewed, the old ways of thinking will be cut off by this sharp sword of God's Word, and what remains will be God's truth, guiding you into true prosperity.

CHAPTER FIVE

Sowing and Reaping

HAVE YOU EVER WATCHED a farmer working a field on a sunny spring day filled with promise? Before him is spread acre upon acre of rich, dark, fertile soil ready to do what God created it to do: bring forth a harvest. As this craftsman of the earth goes about his work, turning row after row of long straight furrows of blank soil, in his mind's eye he carries a distinct image of the reward that will be his a few short months ahead, as the flat, drab field of earth is gradually transformed into a vast colorful landscape of golden waves of wheat or tasseled corn, spreading out in the autumn sun as far as the eye can see, ripe and ready for harvest.

For countless generations those who till the soil have gone about their springtime work in much the same way. While yesteryear's simple stone or steel plow pulled by oxen or horses have been replaced by high-tech diesel tractors and complex cultivating machinery, the task of the farmer still breaks down to a few basic steps: breaking up the fallow ground, carefully preparing the soil for planting, sowing the seed in hope and expectation—and waiting for the harvest.

The farmer knows that if he has followed the proper procedure—the same one his father and his father's father followed before him—staying patient with weather, time, and other factors, he will reap the fruit of his labors.

SOWING TO THE FLESH—OR THE SPIRIT

Since time began those who cultivate the land have followed a divine principle of sowing and reaping that God designed in His creation of this earth. That principle is stated simply in Genesis 8:22: "While the earth remains, seedtime and harvest. . . ." While this scripture states the obvious design of God's handiwork that has been played out on the landscape of earth throughout the ages, there is a profound and dynamic spiritual truth at work in this passage as well. Throughout Scripture God speaks clearly to us about the importance of the seeds we sow throughout our life—and of the harvest we will reap because of them. The seeds we sow include our talents and abilities, our time, our words, our attitudes and actions—and, of course, our finances.

The Bible is clear that in the spiritual realm, there are only two types of ground into which we can sow seed—the flesh and the spirit. Both ground is fertile and ready to receive the seed we will plant, and both will produce an abundant harvest. But how different is the harvest of the flesh from the harvest we will reap when we sow spiritual seeds! Read what the apostle Paul tells us:

> *Do not be deceived, God is not mocked; for whatever a man sows, that he will also reap. For he who sows to his flesh will of the flesh reap corruption, but he who sows to the Spirit will of the Spirit reap everlasting life. (Galatians 6:7-8)*

Remember that as believers each of us will stand before Christ's judgment seat to give an account for what we have done in this life—the seeds we have planted and the harvest that has come from those seeds. Tell me, are you confident that the seeds you are planting now will reap a harvest of "everlasting life"? By that I mean, have you invested that which God has placed in your life—your time, your talents, and your resources—into things that are eternally sound and that will reap a harvest fit for God's kingdom?

Yes, let's talk about money for a minute, because how we use the finances with which God has blessed us tells a whole lot about what we value and the harvest we will reap? Are you sowing the seeds of finance into the good ground of the kingdom of God, into ministries that are winning the lost, equipping disciples for the kingdom, healing the sick, and doing works of justice in your community and around the world? Are your first fruits, your tithes, as well as your offerings going back to kingdom purposes that will last for eternity? Are the hungry being fed, the naked clothed, those in prison visited and encouraged in the Lord? Friend, those are the seeds, sown to the Spirit, that will reap everlasting life. Those are the seeds that will mean untold souls brought to salvation through Jesus Christ.

Perhaps you are taking stock of your eternal "investment portfolio" and find your return thinner than you had hoped. Instead of sowing into God's kingdom, have you found yourself sowing into your own kingdom, "investing" in things that, at the end of the day, will be worth nothing? A newer car, a bigger home, nicer clothes, vacations, a larger savings or retirement account—the list is endless. But the result is the same: you have been sowing to the flesh, and the harvest, God says, will be "corruption"—meaning that everything you thought was yours will one day be burned by God's refining fire.

> ***"... God speaks clearly to us about the importance of the seeds we sow throughout our life—and of the harvest we will reap because of them."***

On that day, when your works are judged against God's perfect and righteous standard, only the gold, silver, and "precious stones" of your eternal seed sown into His kingdom will survive. If you have not invested wisely, following God's firstfruits principle, all you will have for your life's efforts will be what the apostle Paul refers to as "wood, hay, and straw" (1 Corinthians 3:12). Yes, you will be saved, but it will be "as through fire" (1 Corinthians 3:16), as the harvest of your seed, sown to the flesh, is destroyed through God's refining judgment.

FIRST THE SEED, THEN THE HARVEST

Now hear me well. There is nothing at all wrong with owning nice things, of enjoying the fruits of your labors. God desires to bless you with all the good things of His creation. But He will not pour out that blessing in contradiction to His Word. Your first fruits, sown in good ground prepared with faith founded upon God's unchanging Word, must come first, followed by the promised harvest. And that harvest will be an eternal one based on kingdom principles. God desires that many come to salvation through His Son. In fact, His Word says that He is "not willing that any should perish but that all should come to repentance" (2 Peter 3:9). And God has promised that if you will commit to sowing your seed for an eternal harvest, He will also supply "all your need" according to His great riches.

You see, there is an "if, then" concept at work here that believers who wish to be blessed in every realm of life must follow. Let's be clear about kingdom concepts. In every instance there is always a step of faith that we must take, followed by God's response. It begins with salvation, as the Word of God tells us that "if you confess with your mouth the Lord Jesus and believe in your heart that God has raised Him from the dead, you will be saved" (Romans 10:9). There is a two-step process to salvation: believing and confessing.

As it is when we get saved, so it is in every other area of kingdom advance in our lives. We cannot do God's part, and He will not do our part. Our part is responding to His Word, stepping out in faith, and standing on His unbreakable promises. His part is to meet us at our point of need through the power of His risen Son, to be a Father to us, to bring us healing and deliverance through Jesus, to give us a place and a purpose, and to provide us with an inheritance that will not fade away.

In the area of the firstfruits blessing, the same thing goes. You have a part to play in receiving that blessing and God spells it out: "Honor the Lord with your possessions, and with the firstfruits of all your increase..." (Proverbs 3:9). You see, that's not something God will do for you. He wants His children to honor Him and this is one obvious way He has spelled out that we can do that.

AN OVERFLOWING BLESSING

Honoring the Lord with your finances—beginning with the tithe and extending to your freewill offerings—is one crucial way that God has created for you to sow seed that will reap a harvest both now and into eternity. When you sow your finances into vital ministries, when you give to those in need in the limitless ways God has provided for that, you can be assured that God will respond with the harvest, just as He promises in the very next verse of Proverbs 3: "... so your barns will be filled with plenty, and your vats will overflow with new wine" (v.10).

Now to the children of Israel to whom the writer of Proverbs penned this wise counsel, barns that were filled and vats that overflowed with new wine spoke of an abundant harvest right where it mattered. To us it would be like money in the bank, a significant raise at work, or a promotion in a career. To the children of Israel it meant that they would have plenty to eat, sufficient crops and wine to sell for money, and the discretionary income to do the things that they had dreamed of doing. But it began by them taking a portion of their grain and wine—the tithe and beyond—to the house of the Lord.

Just like believers today, the children of Israel had experienced lean times that came as a result of not obeying God in this vital area. He had certainly blessed them over and over, and He had given them clear directions for tithing their first fruits. But instead of sowing back to His eternal purposes, many of the children of Israel took what belonged to the Lord and used it on themselves. The Lord said, "you have robbed Me ... in tithes and offerings," and because of it "you are cursed" (Malachi 3: 8-9).

The good news is that God never gave up on His covenant children Israel and He won't give up on those today who have found themselves shortchanging Him of this precious seed of the first fruits. God's counsel today is the same as yesterday:

Turn it around and begin this very day to sow to the heavenlies with the first fruits of all your increase.

His immutable promise is that He will pour out a blessing so large that "there will not be room enough to receive it." Furthermore He promised to rebuke the enemy, whom He calls the "devourer" (v. 11) so that he will be absolutely powerless to steal your expected harvest any longer. Finally, everyone around you will call you blessed, and you will be to them "a delightful land" (v. 12).

Now, you may not feel very delightful right now, and those around you may be pointing the finger as you have suffered under the curse for so long. My word to you, dear brother or sister, is LOOK UP, for your redeemer stands nigh and He will help you now. Your barns will be filled and your vats will absolutely overflow with new wine.

YOUR FIELD OF HARVEST

Now you may say to me, Bishop Fernandez, I don't have a barn, I don't have any vats for wine, and the only overflowing I see are bills pouring out of my mailbox, and debt collectors leaving messages on my phone.

Let me tell you, friend, if you will heed this wise counsel, and begin sowing seed right where you are, you will start to see the overflow, and you won't be able to stop it even if you tried—because you cannot stop God's faithfulness.

Now, you may not have a barn, but you do (or you can) have a bank account. You have a refrigerator, and you have a pantry for all the good things God give us to eat. If you have a job, whether you flip burgers at a fast-food restaurant, clerk at a convenience store, or you have a career that you are happy with and that pays you well—your job represents God's portal for blessing you at this moment.

That is your field for harvest, and every check you receive is an opportunity for you to sow the first fruits of your tithe—and beyond in a freewill offering—back to God's kingdom purposes. Here at The Faith Center the avenues for such sowing are numerous, including evangelism and discipleship, prison ministry, feeding and clothing the needy, reaching out in hope to orphans and troubled youth, and helping them prepare for a life of God's destiny through the University of Fort Lauderdale. And that's just the beginning of what God is doing in our midst!

Think of how God will lovingly use your seed—whether it's a few dollars or hundreds of thousands and beyond—to win sons and daughter to Himself through the blood of Jesus Christ, and further build up a kingdom of priests unto Himself, giving themselves to worshipping Jesus Christ in all His glory for all eternity! How is that for a return on your investment?

And while He is at it, He won't leave you out in the cold, but will make sure that you have all that you need—and more—to fulfill the destiny He has for you. That means that He will meet all your physical needs with the abundance of His storehouse, so that you will have more than enough for yourself and your loved ones.

Let me assure you, God will not be a debtor to any person. He is a gentleman as well as very generous. The writer of Proverbs tells us that the one "who has pity on the poor lends to the Lord, and He will pay back what he has given" (Proverbs 19: 17). And let's not forget "good measure, pressed down, shaken together, and running over" will God give back to you (Luke 6:38).

Now you may feel that you're the poor one who needs the pity. But if you are God's child through faith in Jesus Christ He says something far different. He has the windows of heaven open for you, and He will supply all your needs in a manner that is "exceedingly abundantly above all" that you can ask or think, according to the power that is working in you (Ephesians 3: 20).

Every first fruit seed you sow into His kingdom purposes not only cares for those who are physically poor—in need of clothing, food, medical care, a place to live, and someone to love them into the kingdom. When you give you are also having pity on those who are poor in spirit, and so you become the vehicle of fulfillment of Christ's prophetic declaration: "Blessed are the poor in spirit, for theirs is the kingdom of heaven. Blessed are those who mourn, for they shall be comforted," and "Blessed are those who hunger and thirst for righteousness, for they shall be filled" (Matthew 5: 3, 4, 6).

I highlight just these three verses, but as a giver into God's kingdom, you can count yourself as both a vehicle for God's blessing, as well as one who is abundantly blessed with all the beatitudes (vv. 3-12). Those are weighty blessings and come with some profound and sobering consequences for those who will embrace them, so I invite you to spend some time meditating on them.

THE "NEW WINE" OF HIS HOLY SPIRIT

And what about the vats of new wine that Proverbs promises for us? I believe strongly that for the redeemed through Christ, the new wine represents an overflowing abundance of God's Holy Spirit in us and flowing out of us to the world. Jesus promised that when He went back to the Father, He would send the comforter, the Holy Spirit who would lead us into all truth (John 16:13). We often confine the truth that the Holy Spirit gives us to that which we will find in Scripture alone. When we come to God's Word we ask the Holy Spirit to guide us into the truth so that we can know Jesus better. Of course, this is exactly what we should do. We want to know Jesus more and more, to be conformed to His image, and do the works that He did when He walked the earth.

But Jesus is not confined to the pages of a book. He lives in the real world where we do, and His Holy Spirit is the key person who brings revelation, discernment, and direction to us on every level of our lives. He empowers us to live victoriously, to be salt and light to those around us, to bring the light and power of His presence right to the place where we live, so that through us His kingdom comes, and His will is done, on earth just as it is in heaven.

I am also convinced that the Holy Spirit gives us direction for the prosperity and advance we need to succeed in life. What is it that causes key individuals in God's kingdom to succeed in business where others fail? How is it that just at the right time God opens a door for His servants to succeed with opportunities and ideas? Friend, it is the Holy Spirit giving discernment and direction. God has His hand on His vast treasury, and He is ready, able, and willing to open that treasury to His children if they will just ask Him for direction and revelation about how they can prosper in their realm of influence.

> ***"Perhaps you are taking stock of your eternal 'investment portfolio' and find your return thinner than you had hoped."***

I know of a young man who loved God and had a good head on his shoulders, but struggled financially and hardly had two cents to rub together. But he believed that God had an open door for him and he persevered in prayer, asking God by His Holy Spirit to drop into his heart an idea that would allow him to prosper. One night as he lay sleeping, God literally woke this young man up with an idea that would revolutionize a product that millions of people use all over the world. This man got out of bed, quickly sketched out the idea that the Holy Spirit had dropped into his spirit, and in the days, weeks, and months that ensued patented a design that made him a multi-millionaire.

Today that man not only employs hundreds of individuals, but he pours vast amounts of his wealth back into the kingdom of God, financing soul-winning ventures, giving to those who are in need, and doing the work of the kingdom.

You see, the Holy Spirit became in Him a fountain of living water, an overflowing vat of new wine, that not only benefited him and his family, but has spread out across the earth to bless others and extend the borders of God's kingdom.

The same thing will happen to you as an extension of your firstfruits offering to the Lord. Friend, you are a child of God, with all the rights and privileges that God delineates in His Word. You have the Holy Spirit within you and you have the right—even the responsibility—to ask for the increase of His Holy Spirit to overflow in your life. You have needs and responsibilities that can only be met with supernatural provision. God wants to meet those needs out of His abundant storehouse.

Why not begin today to ask God, by His Holy Spirit, to drop ideas in your heart that will bring prosperity to your household. Ask Him to open the door of opportunity, to give you discernment to recognize those doors, and the boldness to walk through those doors and into your destiny. Believe me, God is no respecter of persons, and what he has done for others He will do for you.

It may be that He has an idea that He is holding in reserve just for you, or an opportunity that He is holding in His hand that He wants to transfer to you. Ask Him for release, for the increase of the power of His Holy Spirit in your life so that you can step into the destiny that He has for you.

When you commit your first fruits to Him, not only will He supernaturally provide for your needs, but He will arrange your circumstances so that you will have favor in the right arenas, and prosperity will come your way.

DON'T GET WEARY!

As God prospers you it is important to keep on acknowledging His hand of blessing in your life and not grow complacent and begin to think that it is your own power and abilities that have prospered you. An important principle of first fruits giving is that every good gift we receive comes from Him, and so even what we have must be committed to Him with an attitude of humility. Too many of God's people seem to have a "what's mine is mine" mentality about their possessions—including their financial resources—and so it is difficult for God to truly get hold of their hearts so that He can move the blessing through them, and then get it back to them. One of the foundational principles of being truly blessed in God's kingdom is this: God will have no trouble piling blessing upon blessing upon you, once He has determined that He can use you as a conduit to get the blessing to others.

The problem, however, is that many believers want an immediate payoff for the seeds they sow, an instant return rather than, like the farmer, doing the diligent work that will guarantee an abundant harvest. That means preparing the ground, planting the seeds, and then waiting expectantly for the harvest that God has promised.

The apostle Paul encourages us not to "grow weary while doing good, for in due season we shall reap if we do not lose heart" (Galatians 6:9). This means that when we sow to the Spirit, as God commands, we must persevere in order to see the harvest we desire.

The truth of the matter is God's season and your season may be different. But you can rest in the assurance that God is never late, but always on time in bringing the harvest for which you are believing. In the midst of economic turmoil there are multitudes of Christians who need a financial breakthrough. They are giving diligently of the first fruits of all their increase, and even going beyond to the place of extravagant giving in their own time of need. They have caught the vision of souls brought into the kingdom of God, of believers discipled and brought to maturity, of men and women equipped for the work of the gospel, and then released into the kingdom destiny for which God created them.

To them God has promised that in the "due season" of His perfect timetable they will reap the abundant harvest. What does that mean for your season of sowing and reaping? Perhaps your "due season" will mean rapid return on the sowing of your seed. Or maybe you will find it necessary to wait in faith, declaring God's goodness over your situation for a length of time.

When you stand on God's Word, trusting in His timing and purposes, He will bring the harvest at just the right time to meet your needs according to His riches in glory. When you plant good seed in the good ground of God's kingdom, you will reap a rich harvest of God's goodness.

Do not grow discouraged as you wait for your season of personal harvest and destiny. Persevere in the things that God has put before you. Stay in the Word, pray in the Spirit, refuse to doubt or complain in the place of adversity. Your faithfulness to the simplicity of trusting God will ensure that you win.

YOUR ENTIRE LIFE IS A SEED

Remember that it is not only your seeds of finances that matter. You should consider your entire life a seed that is to be sown into the fertile soil of God's kingdom. As you give of yourself willingly as an offering to God, dying to your own ambitions and desires and putting Him first, you will position yourself to reap a rich harvest of God's blessings both in this life, as well as in eternity. You see, it is impossible to produce the kind of fruit God created you to give until you come to an end of yourself and give away that which is precious to you—your very life—as an offering to God. That is what it means to die to yourself. That is what Jesus did in every way for us, laying aside His divinity, taking the form of a slave, dying for you and me, and relying on the power of God to raise Him up in resurrection power. As you give yourself to Christ through loving Him, continuing in obedience to His Word and seeking for His kingdom to be advanced in whatever ways He opens to you, you will reap a great harvest.

And yes, as you focus your heart and mind on loving God, you will find the vital realm of your finances being transformed. That will come from looking to Him as your source and trusting in Him fully for your every need. Friend, I believe strongly that in the days ahead, as our economy is shaken and the world is thrown more and more into confusion, God's children can be positioned to enjoy a place of refuge in His provision for them, because they are trusting in Him and not in their own abilities. They will have learned the secret of casting all their care upon Him knowing that He cares for them.

> ***"...every good gift we receive comes from Him, and so even what we have must be committed to Him with an attitude of humility."***

I believe that much of the shaking the world has been facing over the last few years, and which has touched God's people as well, has been for the purpose of compelling God's people to stop thinking as the world thinks, relying on their own abilities and efforts to see them through the tough times ahead, and instead put their trust wholly in God.

Just as God told His people Israel that it was He who empowered them for wealth (Deuteronomy 8:18), He desires that His people today, those who have put their faith in Christ alone, see Him as their source of provision and prosperity. God said there is coming a day when everything that can be shaken in this world will be shaken, so that only that which is founded upon His unfailing Word will stand (Hebrews 12:27). As that shaking increases over the years ahead—when fear, confusion, and perplexity hold sway in this world as the foundations upon which individuals and nations have relied crumble into dust—God's people will be able to stand upon the rock of His faithfulness while others are swept away.

WE SERVE A GOD OF UNLIMITED RESOURCES!

Never forget, dear child of God, that your heavenly Father has unlimited resources, that there is no lack in His ability to care for you in every way. The reason He calls us to tithe—to give of the first fruits of all that we earn—is not for Him, but for us. Tithing a representative portion of what we have—no matter how small or large it is—offers us an opportunity to step out in faith and declare: "Father, I know that everything that I have comes from your hand alone. You give me the power to earn income, and I am grateful to you for all your provision. I place my first fruits in your hand with faith that you will prosper me and open up opportunities for me to have the abundance that I need. My first fruits offering to you is my step of faith that you are going to pour out a blessing on me that I will not be able to contain."

Friend, simple faith is all it takes to step into that place of abundance God desires for each of us. You see, prosperity represents so much more than having financial provision, as important as that is to us. True prosperity goes all the way to the calm assurance that God will provide for all of our needs according to His riches in glory—no matter what our circumstances look like. That is what enabled the apostle Paul to declare:

> *...I have learned in whatever state I am, to be content: I know how to be abased, and I know how to abound. Everywhere and in all things I have learned both to be full and to be hungry, both to abound and to suffer need. I can do all things through Christ who strengthens me. (Philippians 4: 11-13)*

As difficult as this is to believe, this declaration by Paul represents what it really means to enjoy God's fullness and abundance in this earth. We are truly prosperous when He becomes to us the sum total of all we desire in life—when He becomes both our provider and our provision. Scripture tells us that God humbled the children of Israel and led them through the wilderness for 40 years, feeding them miraculously for many years on manna, so that He could show them that "man shall not live by bread alone; but man lives by every word that proceeds from the mouth of the Lord" (Deuteronomy 8:3).

During all that time not only did they never suffer hunger, God's Word recounts that their clothing never wore out, nor did their feet swell, because God went before them and tenderly cared for them.

It is important for you to know that God cares every bit as much for you as He did for the children of Israel. You are just as much His covenant child as they were, because Jesus has brought you into God's household. His miraculous provision are just as much in operation as they were for Israel as they wandered through the wilderness.

Your commitment to the principle of firstfruits giving represents a step of obedience to God's Word that will bear abundant results in His provision in your life.

CHAPTER SIX

Giving Extravagantly

THROUGHOUT THIS BOOK we have been discussing the priority God places on His people giving of the first fruits of their increase. "Bring all the tithes into the storehouse," God commands, and as we have seen, His promise is great. He challenges us to "try Me now in this . . . if I will not open for you the windows of heaven and pour out for you such blessing that there will not be room enough to receive it" (Malachi 3:10).

God promises us that as we give into His kingdom, beginning with the tithe, we will always have an abundance of what we need for the purposes to which He has called us. And as we have seen, He is calling us on to ever higher plateaus of faith. God wants us to step out, step up, and move on in the unlimited grace that He has for us, and one practical way in which we can stretch ourselves to receive that grace is through our giving.

"SEED TO THE SOWER"

He promises that if we sow bountifully of our resources, then we will reap bountifully, not just in financial and material blessings, but in kingdom advance. Perhaps you haven't put a great deal of thought into this, but how would you respond to God's invitation to give if you knew that every dime you sowed into His kingdom would come back in souls saved, individuals healed and delivered, the needy fed and clothed, and God's righteousness extended to the furthermost parts of the earth? Friend, take a look at what the apostle Paul, through the unction of the Holy Spirit, tells us about the impact of our giving:

> *Now may He who supplies seed to the sower, and bread for food, supply and multiply the seed you have sown and increase the fruits of your righteousness, while you are enriched in everything for all liberality, which causes thanksgiving through us to God. (2 Corinthians 9:10–11)*

Do you see the cause and effect that God puts into action by the power of His Holy Spirit as we embrace His economic model? First, we acknowledge that He is the suppler of both the seed we sow and the harvest we reap. Nothing happens without His hand of blessing. Next, we get a revelation of the wonderful truth that out of His goodness He will take the seed He gives to us, and as we partner in His purposes, He will respond by incrementally increasing both what we sow and the subsequent harvest, so that there will be a perpetual cycle of God-anointed sowing and reaping—all of which will result in an unending harvest of righteousness and thanksgiving to God.

And friend, while it all starts with the tithe, I am convinced that is just the beginning—the starting point for God's blessing. Everything I read in Scripture indicates that the more we give, the more we are empowered by God to bless—and to be blessed—both now and in eternity.

ABOVE AND BEYOND

I truly believe that God created us to be extravagant givers, just like He is. His desire is that we be "pressed down, shaken together, and running over" people, pouring our time, talents, and resources into His kingdom, and in return receiving an abundance of both material blessing and Holy Spirit power and authority to impact our place and purpose—the realm of influence to which He has called us.

Friend, God truly wants you to have an "abundance for every good work" (2 Corinthians 9:8). When you give the tithe—the first ten percent of your income—to the house of the Lord as He commands, He will empower you to use the remaining ninety percent in a manner you would not have been able to accomplish otherwise. That ninety percent will actually go farther than the one hundred percent you would have had without giving to God.

I believe that one reason God does this is so that we get a little "ten percent" taste of the blessings He has for us if we will just trust Him. You see, He wants us to go so much farther, into the realm of extravagant worship to Him through our offerings. He really does wants us to try Him, to test Him in this realm of our lives, to prove Him faithful in His promise to outgive us to a maximum level, so that the blessing will be more than we can even receive. Out of that overflow of blessing He desires us to give back again.

In short, I believe the command to tithe is an invitation from God for us to step out "over the line" into a place of deeper devotion to Him in our finances, trusting His leadership and direction, keeping an ear open for the voice of His Holy Spirit as He directs our steps in giving—and receiving.

"God wants us to step out, step up, and move on in the unlimited grace that He has for us. . . ."

Someone once said that in the life of the believer, money is either a tool or an idol—a blessing or a curse. God is looking for those few who will tear down that idol in their lives, break the curse that keeps them in bondage, and allow Him to be the Lord in this area. Yes, it is a difficult issue, and, of course, God has grace to see each of us through to victory. He doesn't want any of His children to be enchained by the spiritual bondage that comes when money controls our motivations.

He understands much better than we ever will that this last, great fortress of selfishness and fear does not come down easily in the lives of most people. Each of us must make a conscious commitment, through the power of the Holy Spirit, to allow Christ to come in and take ownership of our finances. How blessed and empowered for kingdom advance do you think you would be if you were one of the relatively few to whom God could come at any time, ask you to give into a need—no matter how small or big—and you would respond?

"TO WHOM MUCH IS GIVEN..."

In Luke 12:42, Jesus asks, "Who then is that faithful and wise steward, whom his master will make ruler over his household...?" Those words "faithful and wise" really reflect what God is seeking in those who will respond well in the area of their finances. All of God's people are called to stewardship in this area—regardless of how much God has given them to work with—but not everyone will rise to that level of faithfulness and wisdom that God requires of those whom He can trust with great financial prosperity.

In this same passage Jesus declares: "Blessed is that servant whom his master will find so doing when he comes. Truly, I say to you that he will make him ruler over all that he has" (vv. 43-44).

Recall, as we discussed earlier in this book, that each of us as Christians will have to give an account for the deeds we have done on earth. Yes, we are saved by Christ's blood, but we will still be judged by how well we completed the assignment we were given to do by God—the extent to which we accomplished those tasks that He placed before us.

Take a moment to think about this crucial issue of wise stewardship in an intensely personal way. When you stand before the judgment seat of Christ, what will be His verdict on how well you reached out to your loved ones, friends, and neighbors with the love of Christ? How prayerfully concerned were you about showing forth an impacting testimony of Christ's transforming power on the job, at school, and in your community? As a parent did you pastor your children in such a way that they grew up understanding and embracing the fear of God and His Lordship in their lives?

What will Jesus say to you about your use of the time, talents, and abilities with which He entrusted you? And in the crucial area of finances, will He say "well done good and faithful servant," or will you stand ashamed as He reveals how foolishly you squandered the precious resources with which He blessed you?

As children of God redeemed through Jesus Christ we are called to a higher standard of attitude and action. Jesus said that the one "to whom much is given, from him much will be required" (Luke 12:48). When He gave His one and only Son for our salvation, God poured His all into our lives. When He tells us that He will supply all of our needs according to His riches in glory by Christ Jesus, He means that all of our needs are covered by His grace.

Because of this great grace poured out to us, God does not want us fixated and fretting on this aspect of life. We don't have to be concerned about the necessities of life, because "your heavenly Father knows that you need all these things" (Matthew 6:32). Instead, we are to "seek first the kingdom of God and His righteousness," knowing that all the things we have need of will be richly supplied to us (v. 33).

How does this play out in the realm of finances? It is simple! Whether we have little or much, God wants us to be focused on Him—loving Him, seeking His kingdom, and doing His will "on earth as it is in heaven" (Matthew 6:10).

EMBRACING A LIFESTYLE OF SIMPLICITY

Friend, I believe that we are heading into one of the most intense periods the Church has ever witnessed, both in terms of the persecution of the saints and the opportunity for bringing unprecedented numbers of souls into God's kingdom. I believe that God is going to pour out great wealth for the purpose of this time of harvest, and He is looking for individuals He can trust to steward these resources wisely into His purposes.

Even now we are witnessing a major shift in the body of Christ, as more and more believers embrace a lifestyle of simplicity, committing to living on less for themselves so they can pour more of their finances into the work of the kingdom. They are downsizing their homes, driving more modest vehicles, sacrificing expensive toys, vacations, and luxuries they might once have considered essential for fulfilling their version of the "American Dream."

Instead of giving ten percent of their income and living on the remaining ninety percent, there is a whole group of Christians all over the nation and the world to whom God has been speaking about giving more—about becoming truly extravagant in their offerings to Him.

Yes, by His Holy Spirit God is empowering a whole generation of His people for great wealth, and many are responding by saying, "God I don't want to give you ten percent. I want to give you fifty, sixty, seventy—even ninety percent, and I will live on the rest."

"Whether we have little or much, God wants us to be focused on Him...."

And God is responding with an astounding measure of His grace toward these individuals who are stepping out in faith, causing their offerings to shake the world for His kingdom through a harvest of individuals coming to faith in Christ, churches started, and universities and ministry training centers funded to equip and send out workers into the harvest. Furthermore, all over the world individuals and communities are being impacted by those who have the heart of the Father—a giving heart—to reach out and meet people right where they are hurting and in need.

WHERE IS YOUR TREASURE?

Scripture tells us that "the eyes of the Lord run to and fro throughout the whole earth, to show Himself strong on behalf of those whose heart is loyal to Him" (2 Chronicles 16:9). How rare it is in this world to find an individual who gives himself wholeheartedly to the Lord, to put Him and His interests first and foremost in life. Most Christians would say that this is their heart's desire, but in the everyday hustle and bustle of living the priorities of the kingdom often go to second place. This is so very evident in the area of finances. Making a living, paying bills, and ensuring a lifestyle of comfort and leisure end up taking precedence in the lives of many people, because that is what the world emphasizes as most important.

If you want to see where a person's heart really is, take a look at how he or she relates to money. Jesus made this abundantly clear when He spoke about treasure. "Do not lay up for yourselves treasures on earth," Jesus said, "but lay up for yourselves treasures in heaven. . . . For where your treasure is, there your heart will be also" (Matthew 6:19-21).

Truly, particularly here in America so many of God's people have spent their lives accumulating "treasure" that will have absolutely no value when their time on earth is finished. By contrast, Jesus is calling us to seek and find treasure that will never fade away, through loving Him and loving others into the kingdom.

In our culture, prosperity and abundance represent a huge status symbol. The car you drive, the size of your home and how nice it is inside and out, the clothes you wear—all of this goes to defining individuals, and we spend an inordinate amount of our time, effort, and money trying to maintain the trappings of this standard. In fact, it becomes a full-time occupation for many individuals today, including more than a few of God's people.

But that is not the common denominator for success in God's economy. When you were born you came here empty-handed, and when you leave you will do the same. Your successes and failures, your accomplishments, your blessings, your abundance, your prosperity, and what you do with all of that—will all remain between the start and finish line of your life's course when you leave this world and go to your eternal reward. Only the treasures you have stored up in heaven—loving God and making Him your one thing, loving others and making them your priority, bringing souls into the kingdom and giving God the glory—only those eternal riches will remain for you to enjoy and relish around the throne of God, laying them at His feet.

That is why the apostle Paul counsels that "having food and clothing, with these we shall be content," (1 Timothy 6:8), warning us that those who make wealth their aim and focus are setting themselves up for destruction. Make no mistake, God does want to prosper His people abundantly above all that we can ask or think. But He wants to do it so that we will give that abundance back to Him through pouring our finances into His kingdom purposes.

A GREAT TRANSFER OF WEALTH

In Proverbs 13:22, God tells us that "the wealth of the sinner is stored up for the righteous." I have often heard believers quote this scripture in the context of their own needs, and really God has no problem with that. He will indeed use the wealth the wicked have stored up for themselves and for their own evil lusts, and transfer it to His kingdom for the needs of His own people. After all, it all belongs to Him anyway.

But there is a far more phenomenal and impacting significance behind this powerful scripture and it is this: God is even right now in the process of positioning people and events to transfer the wealth of this world into the hands of His people for a final global harvest and to display His glory throughout the earth. That's Right! The Lord is preparing to pour the wealth and abundance of the wicked into the lives of those of His people He can entrust with great wealth—all for the purpose of bringing souls into the kingdom and to make His Name glorious throughout the earth.

Are you one of those people God can entrust with great wealth? Where are your priorities? Are you distracted by the cares of this world and by the pull of riches? Or has God given you the revelation that he blesses His people financially so that they can pour it back into His plans and purposes?

If you need that revelation to become a reality in your life, ask Him for it. Spend time in the secret place pouring your heart out to Him concerning this great issue of the heart. If you find that your motives and your focus have not been submitted to His Lordship, simply repent and ask Him by the power of His Holy Spirit to make the necessary change in your attitude and heart to transform you into one of those extravagant givers He is looking for.

EXTRAVAGANT GIVING MEANS SACRIFICE

Remember, being an extravagant giver into God's kingdom has nothing to do with how much money you have to give to the Lord. It is all about the state of your heart. When the poor widow came into the synagogue to give her offering to the Lord, she was surrounded by wealthy people scurrying busily past her to drop in significant offerings. As Jesus observed this scene, He did not focus on those wealthy individuals because He knew that they were giving a small percentage out of their vast wealth. Instead, He immediately saw the heart of this little lady who put in a seemingly insignificant two mites—or, in our economy, about a dollar or so. As she did so He pointed her out to His disciples and declared, "Truly I say to you that this poor widow has put in more than all; for all these out of their abundance put in offerings for God, but she out of her poverty put in all the livelihood she had" (Luke 21:3-4).

You see, this poor woman was truly an extravagant giver. While the other individuals gave out of the extra they had left after their needs were met, what the widow offered to the Lord cost her a great deal—because it was her entire livelihood.

There is a story in the Old Testament that tells of David's desire to purchase a plot of land so that he could build an altar on which to give an offering to the Lord. But the man who owned the land did not want to sell it to David. He wanted to give it to him free and clear. Now you might think this was too good an offer for David to pass up. After all, he was getting the land for free and he could still build the altar and make the offering unto the Lord. This was a sweet deal!

"Are you one of those people God can entrust with great wealth?"

But that was not David's attitude. He insisted upon purchasing the property, telling this well-intentioned man that "I will surely buy it from you for a price; nor will I offer burnt offerings to the Lord my God with that which costs me nothing" (2 Samuel 24:24). And with that David purchased the land for a truly significant price.

You see, a lifestyle of abandoned heartfelt worship to God 24 hours a day, seven days a week will cost you something. Why is it that we are so willing to commit ourselves to the pursuit of excellence in school, in sports, in our careers, putting in years and tens of thousands of dollars to be the best we can be—but when it comes to the house of the Lord we think it is okay to give second best?

When God gave the law about the kind of sacrifice the priests were to offer Him for the sins of the people, did He say it was okay to give second best? After all, it's the thought that counts, right? When the tabernacle was being constructed, and the implements for worship being made, did He allow just any amateur to do the work? No, He commanded that the most skilled craftsmen, working with the finest of materials, do their very best to make the finest for His great plan. Mediocre would not do.

OUR GOD IS A CONSUMING FIRE

Why was it that Ananias and Sapphira were struck dead when they brought their offering and put it at the feet of the apostles (see Acts 5)? No, it wasn't because of the type of gift they gave, but it was their motive. Acting as if they were giving the very best they had, this couple instead gave second best. In fact, the apostle Peter asked them, in effect, "Are you giving your best?" to which they relied, "Yes, our very best." They lied to the Holy Spirit and were struck dead as a result.

Friend, in this day and age we as Christians are standing before the same God who judged this New Testament couple. Scripture tells us that He is a consuming fire whom we must worship with reverence and holy fear (Hebrews 12:28-29). Dare we give less than our best to Him? Dare we continue in our charade of being extravagant givers into the heart of His work, when we are really only giving the remainders and remnants of the blessings He has given to us? I say that it is time for the people of God to come up to a higher standard. Yes, begin with the tithe, pay the tenth, give of your first fruits. But let that be only the beginning!

BEGIN WHERE YOU ARE

Now hear me. I am not saying that God expects you to start at the top of the heap and strive to do something you are not able to accomplish. Friend, we serve a God of grace and mercy. He knows how far you are able to stretch in this grace of extravagant giving to which He is calling each of us. I believe that if you will ask Him He will empower you to increase your giving. And have no doubt—that increase will result in fruit for the kingdom as well as blessing for your household. God has promised it and He cannot lie.

I want to encourage you right now to ask God where to begin in this adventure of becoming an extravagant partner in His kingdom purposes. No matter whether you are barely making ends meet, or you are a multi-millionaire with an abundance of extra income to give, God wants to stretch your vision and allow Him to be the Lord of your finances. Remember, just as the apostle Paul tells us, the same God who provides you with the seed to sow, will multiply that seed both for His purposes and yours, making sure you have all you need.

Begin even now to ask God how much "seed" He wants you to sow beyond your tithe, and where He wants you to place that seed. Remember, you cannot produce fruit if you do not sow the seed. If you sow sparingly in comparison to how much you have, you will reap sparingly. But if you sow bountifully you will reap the same. The point is to begin sowing your seed now so that at the end, when you stand before God, you will have a rich history and heritage that He will honor.

GOD'S MERCY AND BLESSING

In Psalm 67, King David prays a beautiful prayer that I believe offers us a picture of what the motivation should be behind our giving:

> *God be merciful to us and bless us, and cause His face to shine upon us, that Your way may be known on earth, Your salvation among all nations. (Psalm 67:1–2)*

You see, David asked God for blessing so that he could give more into God's kingdom, so that God's ways and purposes could be known on earth.

David goes on to declare:

> *Let the people praise You, O God; Let all the peoples praise You. Then all the earth shall yield her increase; God, our own God, shall bless us. God shall bless us, and all the ends of the earth shall fear Him. (vv. 5–7)*

Praise causes increase, worship brings the blessing. When we bring a sacrifice of worship and praise to the Lord, God causes

His glory to go forth and bring about kingdom expansion. A big part of that sacrifice is our financial worship. There is no greater measure of our sacrifice in worship to the Lord than how we give our money.

Friend, God is pleased when you desire to go to a higher level in your walk with Him. If you will ask the Lord to release the grace for giving upon you, He will. If you will commit never to go back to a lower level, but constantly stretch to expand your giving to 15 percent, to 20 percent, to 30, 40, 50 percent, and beyond, He will release that grace.

Yes it will cost you something. I believe in giving extravagantly He will call you to live more simply, to decrease the extravagance of your own personal lifestyle so that you can pour your resources into what really matters. That doesn't mean living like a pauper. In fact, you will find that your lifestyle is more comfortable than ever, and the material things with which God blesses you will have more meaning and significance than what you strived to maintain when you lived at that lower level.

As we close this book, I want to pray for you, that God would, indeed, pour out His grace upon your life, so that you will be one of those special people of God to whom He can entrust great wealth—so that through you the kingdom of God will come in your realm of influence.

Father, thank You for promising to provide for the needs of Your people above and beyond what we could even ask or think. Thank You for supplying all of our needs according to Your riches in glory by Christ Jesus. I ask now that You would empower my brothers and sisters reading this book to become committed, extravagant givers into Your purposes, beginning with the first fruits of all that You give them, and extending to ever greater heights of faith for giving. Lord, Your Word says that it is You who gives us the power to get wealth—and that it is not our own ingenuity and wisdom. Empower us today for kingdom prosperity, so that out of the abundance that You give us, souls may be saved, people equipped and released into the work of the kingdom, the hungry fed and clothed, the orphans and widows taken care of, and the greatness and glory of Your Name go forth for all eternity. Give us, Father, grace to give large into your purposes. In the Name of Jesus we pray—Amen.

Additional books from Henry Fernandez Ministries

to strengthen your faith and help you fulfill your God-given destiny.

Prayer: The Power Connection

You can plug into the awesome power God has for every Christian. Using the Lord's Prayer as a model, Henry Fernandez teaches how Holy Spirit-empowered prayer will usher in the miraculous in your life. *Prayer: The Power Connection* will make a dramatic difference in your personal prayer life—and in the lives of those for whom you pray. Read it, believe it, and get connected!

Beyond Passion: How to Successfully Handle the Pressures of Dating

How can Christian singles successfully handle the immense pressures of dating and relationships? In *Beyond Passion*, Henry Fernandez offers practical, scriptural instruction on dating, how to defuse the "biological hand grenades" that threaten your purity, and how to deal with the five most prevalent pressures facing singles today.

Breaking the Curse, Unleashing the Blessing

If, as the apostle Paul tells us in Galatians, we are blessed with all the abundant blessings that God promised to Abraham, then why do so many Christians continue to live under the curses of poverty, sickness, broken relationships, and other crushing problems? In *Breaking the Curse, Unleashing the Blessing*, Henry Fernandez lays out the scriptural foundation for the spiritual warfare in which every Christian must aggressively engage in order to destroy the works of Satan and assure success, blessing, and victory in every area of life.

Love The First and Greatest Commandment

Jesus said that the greatest commandments are to love God—and then to love others. In his powerhouse book *Love: The First and Greatest Commandment*, Henry Fernandez takes us through key New Testament passages to demonstrate why divine love must be our top priority. In a world growing darker and colder towards faith, the only way to reach the lost is to love them into God's kingdom.

Faith, Family, and Finances: Strong Foundations for a Better Life

After generations of abundance, America is now staggering under a heavy load of debt and despair brought on by years of greed, idolatry, and immorality. In this powerful book, Henry Fernandez shows how Christians can lead the way back to God's blessing by using His Word to rebuild the foundations of their faith, their families, and their finances.

Pursuing a Lifestyle of Prayer and Fasting

In this timely book that every Christian should read, Henry Fernandez shows how embracing a lifestyle of fasting and prayer will take you past your own weakness and into a place of deep intimacy and strength in Jesus Christ, empowering you to stand in faith for answers to the deepest needs of you and your family, your church and community, your nation, and the world!

For these and other resources from Henry Fernandez Ministries, visit

www.henryfernandez.org

University of Fort Lauderdale

Training and Equipping Tomorrow's Leaders Today

We are a premier Christian university
educating 21st century leaders to reach and restore the
world for Jesus Christ through higher educational degrees
rooted in biblical principles and academic excellence
in an innovative Christian learning environment.

At University of Fort Lauderdale we offer four degree program:

— *Associate of Arts in Business Administration* or
Associate of Science in Ministry —

— *Bachelor of Arts in Business Administration* or
Bachelor of Science in Ministry —

— *Master of Science in Ministry* —

— *Doctor of Science in Ministry* —